GLOBAL TEAMWORK
THE RISE OF COLLABORATION IN
INVESTIGATIVE JOURNALISM

The Reuters Institute for the Study of Journalism at the University of Oxford aims to serve as the leading international forum for a productive engagement between scholars from a wide range of disciplines and practitioners of journalism. As part of this mission, we publish work by academics, journalists, and media industry professionals focusing on some of the most important issues facing journalism around the world today. All our books are reviewed by both our Editorial Committee and expert readers. Our books, however, remain the work of authors writing in their individual capacities, not a collective expression of views from the Institute.

GLOBAL TEAMWORK
THE RISE OF COLLABORATION IN INVESTIGATIVE JOURNALISM

Edited by

RICHARD SAMBROOK

Published by the Reuters Institute for the Study of Journalism,
Department of Politics and International Relations, University of Oxford,
13 Norham Gardens, Oxford, OX2 6PS Tel: 01865 611080

http://reutersinstitute.politics.ox.ac.uk

Published in 2018 by the Reuters Institute for the Study of Journalism
www.reutersinstitute.politics.ox.ac.uk

Copyright editorial selection © 2017 Richard Sambrook
Copyright individual chapters © 2017 Charles Lewis, Brigitte Alfter, Nicolas Kayser-Bril,
Anne Koch, Jan Clements

ISBN: 978-1-907384-35-6

A full CIP record for this book is available from the British Library and Legal Deposit
Libraries

Typeset by Messenger Marketing
www.messengermarketing.co.uk
Printed in Great Britain

Published by the Reuters Institute for the Study of Journalism

Contents

Contributors

Richard Sambrook is Professor of Journalism at Cardiff University and a Senior Research Associate of the Reuters Institute for the Study of Journalism. He was previously a journalist in BBC News for 30 years culminating in a decade on the board of management as Director of News and Director of Global News and the World Service.

Charles Lewis is Professor of Journalism at the American University, Washington, DC. He is a former ABC News and CBS News *60 Minutes* producer who founded The Center for Public Integrity and the International Consortium of Investigative Journalists. He is a MacArthur Fellow and the founding executive editor of the new Investigative Reporting Workshop at the American University.

Brigitte Alfter is Co-founder and Managing Editor of Journalismfund.eu, a support structure for investigative, data and cross-border journalism in Europe. She has been a a freelance journalist based in Copenhagen specialising in European affairs and is a former Brussels correspondent for the Danish daily, Information. She is the author of *The Handbook on Cross-Border Journalism*.

Nicolas Kayser-Bril is a developer and a journalist. He is the CEO and co-founder of Journalism++, a start-up that brings journalists and developers together to rethink journalism. He was previously in charge of data journalism at the Paris-based Owni.fr.

Anne Koch is Program Director for the Global Investigative Journalism Network. Until recently she was a director of Transparency International where she led a partnership with the Organised Crime and Corruption Reporting Project, the Global Anti-Corruption Consortium. Previously she had a 20-year career at BBC News, latterly as deputy director of the English World Service.

Jan Clements is a freelance media legal consultant. Previously she was a senior adviser for editorial legal services, at Guardian News & Media. She provides advice on editorial content and policy issues to a range of bodies including non-profit organisations such as Global Witness (campaigning against global corruption), national newspapers and broadcasters and specialist publishers such as the *British Medical Journal*.

Introduction

Richard Sambrook

Journalism is a business which is naturally competitive. Investigative journalism is an activity which normally seeks exclusivity. However, in recent years we have seen a growth in collaborative investigative journalism – cutting against both these expectations.

This is being driven by a number of factors. First, in the internet age, we are seeing more information publicly available and, for data leaks like Edward Snowden's National Security Agency (NSA) files or the Panama and Paradise Papers, very high levels of material to analyse. This in turn requires specialist expertise which may not be available within every newsroom.

Secondly, set against this, many news organisations have been under severe economic pressure and have fewer resources available to deal with long-term, technically complex investigations. Newsroom staff levels have shrunk as media organisations have come under financial pressure from failing business models, and many traditional news organisations have struggled to invest sufficiently in new technologies or skills. As a consequence, collaboration – by pooling resources and skills – enables news organisations to support investigations they would be unable to conduct alone.

Increased digital competition has meant greater pressure to have impact in a crowded market. High-profile, original investigations can have both brand and commercial benefits. Collaboration – publishing simultaneously globally – can become a story in itself, further increasing the impact of the journalism.

More and more, journalism needs to address pan-national issues including business, politics, energy supply, environmental sustainability, and crime. Accountability journalism, holding the powerful to account, has to cross borders and areas of specialist expertise which challenge the resources available in any single newsroom.

Finally, freedom of expression is under threat in many countries, leading to collaboration as a means of managing exposure and risk. Legal protection unavailable at home may be obtained by running the investigation at arm's length or sharing the risk across a wide range of international players. The case for the value and benefits of accountability journalism has continually to be made, most powerfully by organisations working in concert.

Collaboration is not new. As Charles Lewis reports in the next chapter, in 1846, American newspapers wanted to cover the Mexican border conflict but couldn't afford to go individually so they pooled resources and created what became the Associated Press news agency. Today an organisation like the International Consortium for Investigative Journalists (ICIJ) is a modern catalyst for global investigative journalism, coordinating and nurturing complex stories across countries and organisations.

Much of that has been driven by the series of major data leaks we have seen in recent years. This has been supplemented by a drive towards big data investigations across borders with projects like The Migrant Files from Journalism++ or Laundromat – an investigation into money laundering – from the Organised Crime and Corruption Reporting Project (OCCRP).

Some newspapers, recognising the need to extend beyond their normal boundaries and resources, have launched their own collaborative networks. In 2011, the *Guardian, Le Monde, El País, La Stampa, Gazeta Wyborcza,* and *Süddeutsche Zeitung* joined together under the banner of *Europa* to investigate European issues. In 2015, another group of European publications joined forces to form the European Investigative Collaborations (EIC) group, 'tackling European stories; finding, compiling, processing or analyzing big data-sets; developing under Free Software license our own Network collaborative tools, platforms and information design'.

This study originated from a workshop held at the Reuters Institute for the Study of Journalism at Oxford University in December 2016, which was jointly organised between Rasmus Kleis Nielsen and myself. (The full list of participants is in Appendix 1.) This day-long discussion among journalists directly involved in major investigative collaborations was then supplemented with a number of interviews and by a panel discussion at the Perugia International Journalism Festival in April 2017. This study, consequently, focuses on Europe and the USA. There is much collaboration taking place in Africa, Asia, and South America which was beyond our scope but would undoubtedly merit further research.

These discussions were concerned with partnerships between news organisations and, to some extent, with NGOs. We are not focusing on working with the public in what has been called 'Networked Journalism' or 'Citizen Journalism'. Those have been extensively discussed elsewhere.

Neither do these contributions consider at length the editorial content or ethical issues arising from these leaks. Again, these have been much written about elsewhere. These discussions focused primarily on the mechanics of collaboration, taking as read the justification for publication.

Here we will examine the reasons for increased partnerships in investigative journalism globally. We will look at what supports successful collaboration and at some of the problems and difficulties in managing complex, pan-national and pan-organisation investigations. We hope our conclusions will help others seeking to launch similar complex operations in the future and shed greater light on an important developing approach to accountability journalism.

In Chapter 1, Charles Lewis of the American University in Washington, DC, looks at the history of collaborations in journalism – from news agencies, to computer-assisted reporting in the 1990s to today's data journalism – and explains why they are likely to become an increasingly important feature of investigative journalism as politics and business – and therefore the principle of accountability – becomes pan-national.

In Chapter 2, Richard Sambrook summarises the key editorial issues identified by those involved in the Reuters Institute workshop and International Journalism Festival debate, outlining some of the frameworks within which major investigations have worked.

In Chapter 3, Brigitte Alfter, Managing Editor of the Journalismfund.eu, examines the experiences of those involved in a number of case studies and draws out the skills required to manage a cross-border collaboration, and the importance of a new role: editorial coordinator.

In Chapter 4, Nicolas Kayser-Bril then considers some problems with collaborations and suggests they are to some extent driven by ideology or the wishes of funders as much as by editorial need. He questions whether this is necessarily the right approach to all major data-led investigations.

In Chapter 5, Anne Koch, Program Director, Global Investigative Journalism Network (and former Director of Transparency International), looks at the partnerships between investigative journalists and NGOs and the extent to which boundaries are being blurred as interests align.

In Chapter 6, Jan Clements, a former legal adviser at the *Guardian*, outlines some of the legal challenges to international investigative journalism within UK law and at how legal arbitrage, among other measures, can protect cross-border investigations.

Finally, some conclusions and recommendations are drawn. In summary, these are:

- the need for journalism, particularly accountability journalism, to respond to the new international environment and operations for business, politics, and indeed crime;
- the growing importance of journalism collaborating with expertise beyond the media in delivering accountability in this new environment;
- the need for news organisations to recognise the value of pan-national collaborations and the new skills required to successfully deliver high-profile international investigations.

These skills and new aspects include:

- the importance of team building, establishing trust between partners with clear structures and responsibilities;
- the role neutral intermediaries can play in editorial coordination, communication, and resolving cultural, practice, and priority differences;
- the crucial role of both defensive and offensive technology;
- clarity of purpose with third-party funders and metrics for success;
- and, above all, the importance of advocating the social, political, and economic benefits and value of high-profile investigative journalism.

1

Tear Down These Walls: Innovations in Collaborative Accountability Research and Reporting

Charles Lewis

The future potential for increased collaborative research and journalism is enormous and exciting to imagine. And the dynamics driving the almost boundless 'possible' are the ever-advancing, new computer and other dynamic, related technologies.

Of course, the evolution of communications in general has always been directly related to technological advances, with redounding benefits to the inherently inquisitive professional journalistic, academic and non-government organisation (NGO) research-related communities in particular.

For example, in 1846, combining the low-tech pony express with the invention of the telegraph made it possible for four New York-based newspapers attempting to cover the Mexican–American war to 'actively collect news as it breaks, rather than gather already published news'. And that new technology allowed them to pool their money and send a single reporter to Mexico, his dispatches wired back to them from the closest telegraph office in the US (Alabiso et al. 1998: 173–5). That led to the creation of the Associated Press, an independent, New York-based, not-for-profit, tax-exempt news co-operative that today is the largest and oldest such news-gathering organisation in the world, with 'approximately 1,700 newspaper members, 5,000 radio and television outlets, and 8,500 international broadcasters in 121 countries who received their news in five languages (Dutch, English, French, German, and Spanish)'. It has staff teams in 263 locations worldwide, producing multimedia news content that is 'seen by more than half the world's population every day'.[1]

These kinds of dynamic, technological advances have benefited news organisations throughout the world, including the two other oldest and largest, highly respected, international news services, Reuters (1851) and Agence France-Presse/AFP (1944).[2] In all cases, they have also fostered additional communication and professional collaboration *within* these individual organisations and their far-flung staff personnel but also *outside* with their thousands of 'client' member media organisations, too. Everyone contributes, everyone benefits.

The Associated Press acknowledges that it 'often has the right to use material from its members and subscribers; we sometimes take the work of newspapers, broadcasters and other outlets, rewrite it and transmit it without credit'.[3] And, of course, the individual 'client' news outlets benefit substantially from the national and international news information they cannot otherwise gather for financial and other reasons.

Another, very different kind of US-based, non-profit news organisation, but considerably smaller and younger – begun nearly 150 years later – the Center for Public Integrity (which I founded and began leading in 1989) began exploring journalistic collaborations with news organisations. For example, it had editorial consulting contracts at separate times with two American television network news divisions in the 1990s, in which they could have embargoed, pre-publication access to national news 'findings' from its large, months-long investigations in order to give them time to plan and prepare their broadcast coverage but *not* 'break' it exclusively.[4]

---

[1] Associated Press, https://www.ap.org/about/. Newspaper client numbers, etc., are from an undated website (hence the use of 'approximately'). http://www.encyclopedia.com/social-sciences-and-law/economics-business-and-labor/businesses-and-occupations/associated-press.

[2] Reuters News Agency, https://agency.reuters.com/en/about-us.html. Agence France Presse (FR), https://www.afp.com/en/agency/about.

[3] Associated Press, *News Values and Principles*, https://www.ap.org/about/our-story/news-values.

[4] For more information about the Center for Public Integrity, see: https://www.publicintegrity.org/about and Lewis 2014: 184–215.

Case Study: Investigating State Legislative Ethics Issues in the US

By 1994, the five-year-old, US-based, non-profit, non-partisan investigative journalism organisation, the Center for Public Integrity, decided to expand its national accountability 'watchdog' research/reporting far beyond its base of operations, Washington, DC, to the 'heartland' state of Indiana. Why? Because of the urging of a frustrated local citizen there, who suggested that the Center 'help [journalists] look at their state legislature the same way the Center had examined Washington', with numerous investigations utilising and cross-meshing various primary, government records about the uses and abuses of power (Renzulli and Center for Public Integrity, 2002: 2–3).

Over the next two years, Center researchers obtained and shipped 2,000 pages of paper Indiana state legislative campaign contribution records in Indianapolis, the capital, back to their offices, and

> *painfully typed the records of some [19,000 campaign] contributions into a single database for news organisations to use as a starting point for investigations into the legislature. The hope was that for the first time ever, news organisations across the state [would have] computerised access to campaign records that, up until then, had sat gathering dust in filing cabinets at the state capitol.* (Renzulli and Center for Public Integrity, 2002: 2–3)

The Center made this embargoed information available via individual computer disks to a state-wide consortium of the most respected news organisations in Indiana, including the largest circulation state newspaper, the *Indianapolis Star-News*, the most-watched local television station in Indiana, WTHR-TV (an NBC affiliate television station in Indianapolis), the *Fort Wayne Journal-Gazette*, the *Evansville Courier*, and several other news organisations throughout the state. In addition, the same information was also provided to eight, respected political scientists knowledgeable about state politics at college and universities throughout the state.

Just weeks before joint publication, a day-long, private meeting of all the journalistic and academic individuals involved and their organisations was subsequently held in Greencastle, Indiana (the host site: DePauw University), to discreetly analyse and discuss the major findings and trends from the political influence-related data, first conveyed in a confidential, advisory 60-page Center editorial and methodologically detailed memorandum to all participants, prior to the face-to-face discussion. And a precise, public

7

release date, when every news organisation would begin publishing its stories, was mutually agreed upon and set in February 1996 (Renzulli and Center for Public Integrity, 2002: 2–3).

The resulting, multiple news organisation exposés outraged citizens throughout Indiana. The *Indianapolis Star-News* published a hard-hitting, five-part series of articles titled, 'Statehouse Sellout: How Special Interests Have Hijacked the Legislature', and WTHR-TV aired a multi-day series of stories, 'Legislators for Sale', including a 'confrontational' investigative interview with one of the state legislative leaders. The *Indianapolis Star-News* reported that the state legislators 'wanted to make it tougher to win product liability lawsuits. They got it. They wanted lower wages on public construction projects. They got it. They wanted teacher unions to stop collecting money from non-union teachers. They got that one, too.' According to the newspaper, lobbyists in Indiana 'out-numbered lawmakers by an 8-to-1 ratio. [And] they found lawmakers from both parties who sponsored bills that would help their employees' (Renzulli and Center for Public Integrity, 2002: 3–4).

The public outrage came quickly. In just a few weeks, in the case of just one of the publishing partners, '2,500 angry citizens contact[ed] the *Star-News*' and soon afterwards reform legislation became law 'mandating that all contribution records be made available to citizens online'.[5]

At the same time, of course, not everyone was pleased with the aggressive investigative journalism, particularly the leaders of the Republican-controlled Indiana legislature on the receiving end of the substantial, critical news coverage. But also, less predictably, the then media critic of the *Los Angeles Times*, Eleanor Randolph, criticised the 'outside research' done regarding public state records by the Center for Public Integrity: 'the state media tackled this issue because of outside help... instead of a mystifying flutter of 19,000 paper documents, there was one, tidy computer disk, courtesy of a private, nonpartisan organisation called the Center for Public Integrity'.[6] However, the editor of the *Indianapolis Star*, Frank Caperton, strongly disagreed with her criticism: 'We take information every day from hundreds of people. The real question is the integrity of the information, and Chuck Lewis and his troops met every level of integrity that I know of.'[7]

---

[5] The Center for Public Integrity: Investigative Journalism in the Public Interest (organisation report covering the years 1989–2000), p. 18. https://www.publicintegrity.org/files/manual/pdf/corporate/2000_CPI_Annual_Report.pdf

[6] Eleanor Randolph, 'News Organizations' Use of Outside Research', *Los Angeles Times*, 17 Apr. 1996, http://articles.latimes.com/print/1996-04-17/news/mn-59572_1_news-organizations

[7] Ibid.

In terms of background atmospherics, context, and pushback by politicians, the Center for Public Integrity just *weeks earlier* also had released a highly publicised major national exposé involving the role of money in politics in the 1996 presidential campaign and the 'Top Ten Career Patrons' of every major presidential candidate in both political parties during their respective careers. The book, released days *before* Americans began to cast their votes in the Iowa and New Hampshire and subsequent state caucuses and primaries, was titled *The Buying of the President*. Relatedly, a book-embargoed collaboration with PBS Frontline, a documentary, *So You Want to Buy a President?*, was broadcast at about the same time.[8] And months later, the Center broke the national, Clinton administration 'Lincoln Bedroom' campaign fundraising scandal identifying 75 wealthy donors rewarded with overnight stays in the White House, in an award-winning report entitled *Fat Cat Hotel* (Ebrahim 1996).[9]

A year later, in the considerably more populous and per capita prosperous neighbouring state of Illinois, the Center for Public Integrity 'States Project' team worked with University of Illinois political science professor Kent Redfield, and together they

> *coded roughly 90,000 campaign contributions by industry type so we could determine the state's most influential donors [and] analyzed nearly 23,000 campaign expenditures to find out exactly how state lawmakers spent their money. Because we put [this] database up on our website, for the first time ever, Illinois citizens could find out where state lawmakers got their money with the click of a mouse.*

At least a dozen news organisations throughout the state, including the largest news organisation, the *Chicago Tribune*, aggressively reported on the substantial influence of money there – indeed, 30 front-page news stories

> *hit Illinois newsstands in just one week, informing the citizens of the $73 million that went to state campaigns in the 1996 election cycle. Just four legislative leaders, known as the 'Four Tops,' took in one-third of the total raised and controlled the purse strings of candidates across the state.*
> (Renzulli and Center for Public Integrity 2002: 4)

---

[8] Lewis and Center for Public Integrity 1996. PBS Frontline, '*So You Want to Buy a President?* 30 Jan. 1996. http://www.pbs.org/wgbh/pages/frontline/president/presidentscript.html.

[9] 'Award-winning' refers to the Society of Professional Journalists Sigma Delta Chi Award for Public Service in Newsletter Journalism, given to Margaret Ebrahim.

The first five years of the Center for Public Integrity's data research and reporting collaborations with traditional news organisations tracking state-based campaign finance and political influence and corruption issues, that began with Indiana and then Illinois, culminated in *Our Private Legislatures: Public Service, Personal Gain*. It was a national investigation of conflicts of interest by state lawmakers, displayed on the Center website. That 2000 report was discreetly disseminated in embargoed, pre-publication fashion to a consortium of 50 leading participating newspapers in 50 states. We posted, analysed, and reported on the annual financial disclosure filings of 5,716 state lawmakers throughout the nation, exposing literally *hundreds* of apparent conflicts of interest.[10]

We found, for example, that 41 of America's 50 state legislatures have part-time 'citizen legislators' with other day jobs, but only seven states actually have conflict of interest ethics laws pertaining to their conduct of official business. According to an analysis of financial disclosure reports filed in 1999 by state legislators throughout the US (in 47 of 50 states – three states had no publicly available personal financial disclosure information about lawmakers), Center journalists discovered that 'more than one in five lawmakers sat on a legislative committee that regulated their professional or business interest (in 41 of the 50 states, elected legislators only serve part-time, drawing an average annual salary then of $18,000)'. And at least 18 per cent of the nation's state lawmakers 'had financial ties to businesses or organisations that lobby state government... leav[ing] the public interest to career lawyers, bankers, farmers, lobbyists and insurance brokers in the legislature'.[11]

This was the *first* national investigative journalism about apparent conflicts of interest (or the appearance of what I have called 'legal corruption') in state legislatures and it won the second, annual Investigative Reporting and Editors (IRE) online investigative reporting award. The award judges noted that 'this is the first comprehensive look at all state legislators in one place and the interactive nature of the project allows voters to see for themselves how their lawmakers measure up'.[12]

---

[10] *Our Private Legislatures: Public Service, Personal Gain*, The Center for Public Integrity, 21 May 2000, https://cloudfront-files-1.publicintegrity.org/legacy_projects/pdf_reports/OURPRIVATELEGISLATURES.pdf

[11] Center for Public Integrity, *Investigative Journalism in the Public Interest* (organisation report covering the years 1989–2000), 24. https://www.publicintegrity.org/files/ manual/ pdf/ corporate/2000_CPI_Annual_Report.pdf. Center for Public Integrity, *Our Private Legislatures*.

[12] Investigative Reporters and Editors, Columbia, MO. http://ire.org/awards/ire-awards/winners/2000-ire-award-winners/. Regarding 'legal corruption', see Charles Lewis, 'Legal Corruption and the Mercenary Culture', Invited lecture at the Edmund J. Safra Center for Ethics, Harvard University Law School, 18 Apr. 2013. https://ethics.harvard.edu/charles-lewis-legal-corruption-and-mercenary-culture

That national, state-level scrutiny has continued through the years, with major Center reports in 2004, 2006, and 2009. After these investigative revelations and the ripple effects of local media coverage, 21 states changed their financial disclosure laws, forms, or rules pertaining to lawmakers. Similarly, after the Center exposed the lax disclosure systems in states regarding lobbying, 24 states improved their lobbyist transparency requirements.[13]

But the 2012 States investigation was the largest such effort to date,

> an unprecedented, data-driven analysis of transparency and accountability in all 50 states... a collaboration [between] the Center for Public Integrity, Global Integrity and Public Radio International (PRI), in co-operation with the Investigative News Network (now called the Institute for Non-profit News, INN, comprised of over 100 non-profit news member organisations). Each state received a ranking, based on 330 'Integrity Indicators' in 14 categories, such as access to information, campaign finance and executive accountability, along with others.[14]

The project caught the public's imagination, garnering over 1,200 news stories nationwide, including 89 local public radio stories produced and aired by 16 local public radio stations in California, Washington, New York, Texas, Pennsylvania, Massachusetts, Florida, Colorado, Oregon, North Carolina, Ohio, Missouri, New Hampshire, and Washington, DC. Several states subsequently passed new transparency and ethics-related laws.[15]

Returning to the commercial journalism milieu, inside large news organisations intra- and inter-newsroom, domestic and foreign bureau editorial collaborations also have become substantially more feasible because of the various new media technological advances. And some of the most outstanding public service journalism certainly has benefited enormously from technologically enabled, multimedia collaborations between various news organisation bureaus, as well as editorial coordination and communication on a heretofore unimaginably large scale on important, exceedingly difficult, timely news-making projects.

For example, in the United States, the New York Times won an unprecedented seven Pulitzer Prizes in a single year, 2002 – six of them about

---

[13] Unpublished memo from former Center for Public Integrity director of state projects Leah Rush to Charles Lewis, 27 July 2010.
[14] Center for Public Integrity 2012 Annual Report https://iw-files.s3.amazonaws.com/documents/pdfs/CPI_AnnualReport2012_sm.pdf, p. 7.
[15] Ibid.

the terrorist attacks on 11 September 2001 (in the previous century, no US newspaper had ever won more than three Pulitzer Prizes in a single year).[16] More than 160 *Times* reporters, photographers and editors around the US and the world were involved in the remarkable, herculean daily and long-form media coverage, which included 2,000 brief 'Portraits of Grief' stories chronicling the lives and deaths of the missing at 'Ground Zero' where the attacks occurred, as well as a large, heartrending book with 'charts, graphs and 250 full-color photographs documenting the gripping scenes'.[17]

And in 2010, the *Washington Post* two-time Pulitzer Prize winner Dana Priest and author/journalist William Arkin, both respected national security journalists, and a team of 28 'investigative reporters, cartography experts, database reporters, video journalists, researchers, interactive graphic designers, digital designers, graphic designers and graphics editors' conducted an extraordinary two-year investigation into the US government's nearly decade-long response to the horrific terrorist attacks on 11 September 2001.[18]

The first in a series of investigative articles on 'Top Secret America', was headlined, 'A Hidden World, Growing Beyond Control', and the opening sentence was:

The top-secret world the government created in response to the terrorist attacks of Sept. 11, 2001, has become so large, so unwieldy and so secretive that no one knows how much money it costs, how many people it employs, how many programs exist within it or exactly how many agencies do the same work.[19]

The investigative team learned that 'some 1,271 government organisations and 1,931 private companies work on programs related to counter-terrorism, homeland security and intelligence in about 10,000 locations across the United States', and that in the Washington, DC, area, '33 building complexes for top-secret intelligence work are under construction or have been built since September 2001. Together they occupy the equivalent of almost three

[16] Felicity Barringer, 'Pulitzers Focus on Sept. 11, and The Times wins 7, 9 Apr. 2002. http://www.nytimes.com/2002/04/09/nyregion/pulitzers-focus-on-sept-11-and-the-times-wins-7.html
[17] *New York Times*. Introduction by Howell Raines. *A NATION CHALLENGED: A Visual History of 9/11 and its Aftermath* (New York Times/Callaway, Publishers: New York, 2002).
[18] 'Top Secret America', *Washington Post*, Methodology and credits, http://projects.washingtonpost.com/top-secret-america/articles/methodology/
[19] Dana Priest and William Arkin, 'A Hidden World, Growing Beyond Control', *Washington Post*, 'Top Secret America', 19 July 2010, p. 1. http://projects.washingtonpost.com/top-secret-america/articles/a-hidden-world-growing-beyond-control/

Pentagons or 22 U.S. Capitol buildings'. The reporting/researcher team found that 'many security and intelligence agencies do the same work, creating redundancy and waste. For example, 51 federal organisations and military commands, operating in 15 U.S. cities, track the flow of money to and from terrorist networks.'[20]

Besides the series, their related book, *Top Secret America: The Rise of the New American Security State*, was a national bestseller and it was also accompanied by a PBS Frontline documentary by the same name. The investigative project's methodology was highly sophisticated, and it detailed how they analysed an extraordinarily complex labyrinth of 'hundreds of thousands of public records of government organisations and private-sector companies'. The project team 'scraped' thousands of corporate and local, state, and federal government agency websites, and upon publication, also presented extraordinary, state-of-the-art data visualisation graphics for the reader to better understand the myriad issues involved via straightforward presentations such as 'See the map', 'Explore connections', 'Find companies', and 'Search the data'.[21]

The operative word here is data. Beginning in the 1952 US presidential election with the advent of sophisticated public opinion polling by CBS during elections and other times in the United States which especially accelerated in the 1970s, news organisations were increasingly beginning to realise the critical importance of the need to gather, sort, sift, and analyse massive amounts of computer data in order to better inform their journalism and the public.

A pre-eminent pioneer in 'computer-assisted reporting' has been American journalist Philip Meyer, not only about public opinion research regarding vital matters of the day, but because of a 'seminal book' first published in 1973 and still read by journalists all over the world, *Precision Journalism: A Reporter's Introduction to Social Science Methods*. In it he elucidated a simple but very significant idea, with amplification, 'that journalists should learn adequate research methods from scientists'.[22]

In the United States, the National Institute for Computer-Assisted

---

[20] Ibid.

[21] 'Top Secret America', *Washington Post*, http://projects.washingtonpost.com/top-secret-america/. http://www.pbs.org/wgbh/frontline/film/topsecretamerica/. For information about the book, see https://www.amazon.com/Top-Secret-America-American-Security/dp/B00AF3O2V0.

[22] Gynnild 2014. Biographical information about Philip Meyer, Professor Emeritus at the University of North Carolina, and a video interview with him about his seminal work, Meyer 2002. 'Investigating Power', http://www.investigatingpower.org/ journalist/philip-meyer. Investigating Power is an ongoing, online, multimedia, biographical, and oral history repository about public service journalism in the US since 1950, created and executive-produced by the author. http://investigatingpower.org/about.

Reporting (NICAR, within Investigative Reporters and Editors, IRE, a not-for-profit organisation that is the largest, oldest investigative reporting membership organisation in the world, located at the University of Missouri School of Journalism) was created in 1989. And 'since then, thousands of reporters from the USA and more than 30 other countries have been trained in applying computing to their journalistic activities… and investigative journalists have built their own quantitative databases since the early 1990s' (Gynnild 2014: 718). And every year since 2005, NICAR/IRE presents the prestigious Philip Meyer Award, which 'recognises the best journalism done using social research methods'.[23]

Separately, facilitated because of the evolution of the Web and the computerisation and thus the increased accessibility of government data and other, heretofore paper records, another important development has been 'data-driven journalism'. It is obviously related but somewhat different from 'traditional' computer-assisted reporting because it refers specifically to open data – data that is freely available online and can be analyzed with freely accessible open-source tools. The *Guardian* calls its Content API and Data Store the 'open-platform initiative', and as Astrid Gynnild of the University of Bergen (Norway) has noted, the *Guardian* not only does 'original research on data they have obtained; their Data Blog also provides a searchable index of world government data which contains more than 800 datasets (as of 13 February 2013)' (2014: 719[24]).

No news organisation in the world has advanced open data more than the *Guardian*, which has proudly (and properly) noted that its 'journalists have been working with – and visualising – data since the *Guardian* first published in 1821'. The creator and first editor in 2009 of the online *Guardian*'s internationally popular, daily Datablog website, guardian.co.uk/data, was Simon Rogers, author of *Facts are Sacred: The Power of Data* (2013), who was named the 'Best UK Internet Journalist' by the Oxford Internet Institute at Oxford University. The *Guardian* Datablog is 'the first systematic effort to incorporate publicly available data sources into news reporting', and it is very possibly the 'world's most popular data journalism website'.[25]

---

[23] Investigative Reporters and Editors (IRE). http://www.ire.org/awards/philip-meyer-awards.
[24] Gynnild, Astrid. 2014. 'Journalism Innovation Leads to Innovation Journalism: The Impact of Computational Exploration on Changing Mindsets', *Journalism* 15/6: 713–30
[25] See http://www.multiplejournalism.org/case/the-guardian-datablog; https://www.theguardian.com/news/datablog/ video/2013/apr/04/history-of-data-journalism-video; https://simonrogers.net/about; Peter Kimpton, 'Obama to Berners-Lee, Snow to Domesday: A History of Open Data', *Guardian*, 25 Oct. 2013. https://www.theguardian.com/news/datablog /2013/oct/25/barack-obama-tim-berners-lee-open-data

Of course, the 'biggest news' regarding data and journalism in recent years has been about the unprecedented, massive amounts of leaked secret government data, which have substantially aided and abetted collaboration between competing journalists and their respective news organisations. The three largest, most complex, and controversial, secret leaked 'Big Data' projects ever undertaken and reported by professional journalists in the world, according to *Wired* magazine (and others), have been, in chronological order: (1) Julian Assange-led Wikileaks' 'Cablegate', a 1.73 gigabyte collection of US State Department documents that was 'almost a hundred times bigger' than the leaked US Department of Defense 'Pentagon Papers' (7,000 pages) in 1971, (2) Former National Security Agency (NSA) contractor Edward Snowden's leaks of approximately 1.7 million internal documents, which represents only 15 per cent of the size of (3) the anonymous leak that led to the online publication of the 'Panama Papers: Politicians, Criminals and the Rogue Industry that Hides their Cash' by the International Consortium of Investigative Journalists, which I founded in 1997 as a project within the Center for Public Integrity in Washington.[26]

The Panama Papers leak consisted of 11.5 million documents that belonged to the Panamanian law firm 'and corporate service provider' Mossack Fonseca, including financial and attorney–client information pertaining to over 214,000 offshore entities, including 4.8 million emails about 'how rich and powerful people hide their wealth'. They were anonymously leaked by a confidential source to reporters Bastian Obermayer and Frederik Obermaier at the German newspaper *Süddeutsche Zeitung* and subsequently shared, organised, and published by the International Consortium of Investigative Journalists in Washington.[27] Edward Snowden himself has correctly called the Panama Papers 'the biggest leak in the history of data journalism'.[28]

[26] Andy Greenberg, 'How Reporters Pulled Off the Panama Papers, the Biggest Leak in Whistleblower History', *Wired*, 4 Apr. 2016.
[27] Frederik Obermaier, Bastian Obermayer, Vanessa Wormer, and Wolfgang Jaschensky, 'Panama Papers: The Secrets of Dirty Money', *Süddeutsche Zeitung*, http://panamapapers.sueddeutsche.de/articles/ 56febff0a1bb8d3c3495adf4/
[28] Alan Rusbridger, 'WikiLeaks: The Guardian's Role in the Biggest Leak in the History of the World', *Guardian*, 28 Jan. 2011. https://www.theguardian.com/media/2011/jan/28/wikileaks-julian-assange-alan-rusbridger. https://www.wired.com/2016/04/reporters-pulled-off-panama-papers-biggest-leak-whistleblower-history. Brett Molina, 'Panama Papers vs. NSA: How Big is the Latest Leak?', *USA Today*, 4 Apr. 2016, updated 7:59 a.m. ET, 5 Apr. 2016. https://www.usatoday.com/story/tech/news/2016/04/04/panama-papers-vs-nsa-how-big-latest-leak/82606940/

Case Study: The International Consortium of Investigative Journalists

This investigation has received numerous, prestigious awards around the world, including the Pulitzer Prize for Explanatory Reporting (along with US publishing partners McClatchy and the *Miami Herald*) in the United States. The Pulitzer Prize Board praised the Panama Papers exposé for its collaboration of hundreds of reporters 'on six continents to expose the hidden infrastructure and global scale of offshore tax havens'.[29] According to ICIJ senior editor Michael Hudson, 'in the end, more than 400 journalists – reporters, editors, computer programmers, fact-checkers and others – worked on the project', studied 'millions of confidential emails and corporate documents written in French, English, Spanish, Russian, Mandarin and Arabic and us(ing) shoe-leather reporting to track down additional documents and verify facts on six continents'.[30]

To date, the Panama Papers investigation has prompted over '150 inquiries, audits and investigations in 79 countries and exposed offshore companies linked to more than 150 politicians in more than 50 countries ... including 14 current or former world leaders'. It also has revealed a network of people close to Russian President Vladimir Putin that 'shuffled as much as $2 billion around the world'. And in February 2017, Panamanian government officials arrested the founders of Mossack Fonseca, the Panamanian law firm from which all of the data emanated, for money laundering.[31]

And who was the leaker of the biggest trove of private, sensitive financial and other documents ever revealed? Intriguingly, no one knows, including Bastian Obermayer, the *Süddeutsche Zeitung* reporter at the receiving end of an encrypted email with this tantalising lead: 'Hello, this is John Doe. Interested in data?' Seeking unequivocal anonymity, the leaker set the ground rules: 'My life is in danger, we will only chat over encrypted files.

---

[29] 2017 Pulitzer Prize winner in Explanatory Reporting. http://www.pulitzer.org/winners/international-consortium-investigative-journalists-mcclatchy-and-miami-herald

[30] Michael Hudson, 'Panama Papers Wins Pulitzer Prize', The Global Muckraker/International Consortium of Investigative Journalists, 10 Apr. 2017. https://www.icij.org/blog/2017/04/panama-papers-wins-pulitzer-prize.

[31] Ibid. For more technical details about the Panama Papers collaboration, see Mar Cabra and Erin Kissane, 'The People and Tech Behind the Panama Papers', 11 Apr. 2016. https://source.opennews.org/articles/people-and-tech-behind-panama-papers/. Will Fitzgibbon and Emilia Diaz-Struck, 'Panama Papers have had Historic Global Effects – And the Impacts Keep Coming', 1 Dec. 2016. https://panamapapers.icij.org/20161201-global-impact.html. Will Fitzgibbon, Emilia Diaz-Struck and Michael Hudson, 'Founders of Panama Papers Law Firm Arrested on Money Laundering Charges', 11 Feb. 2017. https://panamapapers.icij.org/20170211-mossfon-panama-arrests.html

No meeting ever.'[32] Obermayer replied, 'We're very interested.' His or her motive was apparently related to income inequality issues, explaining the largest leak in history with this message, 'I understood enough about their contents to realise the scale of the injustices they described.'[33]

The reason the ICIJ could undertake and orchestrate the extensive, indeed unprecedented, global collaboration dissemination of leaked, sensitive financial and other records is because the staff and ICIJ member journalists had navigated similar complex, international financial and tax-related issues for the preceding five years. ICIJ Director Gerard Ryle and Deputy Director Marina Walker Guevara in Washington and Mar Cabra, who is based in Madrid, Spain, and is the Editor overseeing the ICIJ Data & Research Unit, previously had shepherded to international publication with media partners throughout the world other then-unprecedented tax avoidance (legal), evasion (illegal), and 'avoision' (a murky grey area of uncertain illegality or likelihood of government prosecution) exposés also possible because of substantial bank and other leaked data.[34] They included 'Secrecy for Sale: Inside the Global Offshore Money Maze', 'Swiss Leaks: Murky Cash Sheltered by Bank Secrecy', and 'Luxembourg Leaks: Global Companies' Secrets Exposed'.[35]

The massive Panama Papers project was actually the ICIJ's 26th cross-border investigation, and at the time it was published, the ICIJ was a project within the Center for Public Integrity, as it had been since its inception in late 1997. Thus, there was a substantial, 19-year, 25-investigations precedent and logistical and technical learning curve by the organisation and its member journalists leading up to the largest investigative (or any other type of) reporting collaboration in the history of journalism.[36]

---

[32] Juliette Garside, 'Panama Papers: Inside the Guardian's Investigation into Offshore Secrets', *Guardian*, 16 Apr. 2016. https://www.theguardian.com/news/2016/apr/16/panama-papers-inside-the-guardians-investigation-into-offshore-secrets

[33] 'Panama Papers Source Offers Documents to Governments, Hints at More to Come', International Consortium of Investigative Journalists, 6 May 2016. https://panamapapers.icij.org/20160

[34] Biographical information about Gerard Ryle, Marina Walker Guevara, and Mar Cabra: https://www.icij.org/journalists/gerard-ryle; https://www.icij.org/journalists/marina-walker; https://www.icij.org/journalists/mar-cabra. Regarding 'avoision', see Lewis et al. 2001: p. xvii: 'the phenomenon of tax avoidance (that's legal), tax evasion (that's illegal), and tax "avoision" (catch us if you can)'.

[35] International Consortium of Investigative Journalists, 'Secrecy for Sale: Inside the Global Offshore Money Maze' [78 international stories/2013-14], https://www.icij.org/offshore. 'Swiss Leaks: Murky Cash Sheltered by Bank Secrecy' [15 international stories/2015], https://www.icij.org/project/swiss-leaks. 'Luxembourg Leaks: Government Companies' Secrets Exposed' [23 international stories/2014], https://www.icij.org/project/luxembourg-leaks.

[36] International Consortium of Investigative Journalists, https://www.icij.org/projects.

Those prior investigations ranged widely in subject matter from illegal cigarette smuggling by the major tobacco manufacturers; the growing role of private military companies; the privatisation of water on six continents; the international trade in asbestos; the illegal black-market overfishing of the world's oceans; the financial 'windfalls of war' to the private military companies involved in the US wars in Afghanistan and Iraq, etc.[37]

The ICIJ had been created in the autumn of 1997, as an internal project of the Center for Public Integrity, following five full years of exploration, planning, fundraising, etc. The admittedly audacious, even outlandish idea was to create an assemblage of the pre-eminent investigative reporters in the world, who I described jokingly in private as the 'Jedi Knights' of investigative journalism in each of their respective countries around the world. I pondered the possibility and the logistical encumbrances to be surmounted for over five years, personally also convinced that the commercial media organisations would *never* be able to create such a collaborate entity, frankly because of their overweening individual pride, arrogance, competitiveness, and thus their overall inability to 'play in the sandbox with others'.

And at the same time, I was firmly convinced, then and now, as I have noted in the past, that 'amid a world of debilitating political dysfunction with the most dire potential consequences, the crucial concept of public accountability cannot and should not be narrowly confined by local or national borders, or the rigid strictures, orthodoxies, conceits and insecurities of traditional journalism'.[38]

In February 2017, nearly two decades after it had been proposed and had begun as a new project of the Center for Public Integrity, for various reasons the Center and the International Consortium of Investigative Journalists agreed that it was finally time for the latter to become a separate, independent, non-profit news organisation. Incorporated in the United States, at this writing the ICIJ is awaiting formal approval by the US Internal Revenue Service (IRS) of its request to become a 501(c)(3) non-profit, tax-exempt corporation. The Panama Papers global investigation was thus the final ICIJ project published while still a project of the Center.

---

[37] Ibid., and Lewis 2014: 208–10.
[38] Charles Lewis, 'The Future of Journalism in Three Words: Collaboration, Collaboration, Collaboration', 18 Apr. 2016. https://www.theguardian.com/commentisfree/2016/apr/18/future-of-journalism-collaboration-panama-papers

The Promise of Crowdsourcing and Academic–Reportorial Synergies

The relatively recent journalistic application of social science methods more common to academia nationally and internationally has been a *de facto*, implicit first stage in overall collaboration between these important spheres.

From the telegraph to the computer age, the creation of the internet, the World Wide Web, and our brave new world of algorithms, bots, drone journalism, and satellite imagery, etc., what is *already* possible in the 21st century almost defies credulity and it is all moving at lightning speed. Consider that recent, significant phenomena in the context of journalistic application and their linguistic terms such as 'crowdsourcing' and 'Big Data' were not even added to the *Oxford English Dictionary* until 2013![39]

'Crowdsourcing' was first used in print in a *Wired* magazine article in 2006 written by Jeff Howe and edited by Mark Robinson, titled 'The Rise of Crowdsourcing'. And that concept and new word had been inspired in part by an important, well-received 2004 book, *The Wisdom of Crowds*, by James Surowiecki. The meaning of 'crowdsourcing' is, according to Howe in a subsequent online blog, 'the act of a company or institution taking a function once performed by employees and outsourcing it to an undefined (and generally large) network of people in the form of an open call… (a) large network of potential laborers'.[40]

The Columbia Journalism School's Tow Center for Digital Journalism *Guide to Crowdsourcing*, after 51 interviews and analysing 18 survey responses, defines journalism crowdsourcing as 'the act of specifically inviting a group of people to participate in a reporting task – such as newsgathering, data collection, or analysis – through a targeted, open call for input; personal experiences; documents; or other contributions' (Onuoha 2015).

In roughly the past decade, there have been numerous, dramatic, and remarkable examples of the power and rapid evolution of citizen participation in information-gathering, including in the midst of significant national and international 'news' events. Indeed, citizens' involvement in assisting and

---

[39] Mashable, 'Oxford English Dictionary Adds "Crowdsourcing," "Big Data"', http://mashable.com/2013/06/13/dictionary-new-words-2013/

[40] Jeff Howe, 'The Rise of Crowdsourcing', *Wired*, June 2006. https://www.wired.com/2006/06/crowds. Surowiecki 2004. Jeff Howe (blog) 'Crowdsourcing: A Definition', 2 June 2006. http://crowdsourcing.typepad.com/cs/2006/06/crowdsourcing_a.html. It should be noted that in their writings, both Surowiecki and Howe acknowledge they were influenced by a book written 150 years *before* the creation of the World Wide Web, Charles Mackay's *Extraordinary Popular Delusions and the Madness of Crowds*, published in 1841.

contributing to the newsgathering process has been evolving in a dynamic, very engaging way.

For example, on the day of the 'worst terrorist atrocity on British soil', the 7 July 2005 London bombings in which four suicide bombers 'with rucksacks full of explosives attacked central London, killing 52 people and injuring hundreds more', the BBC 'received 22,000 emails and text messages about the bombings and 300 photos, of which 50 were within an hour of the first bomb going off'.[41]

On 13 April 2013 in the United States, two bombs exploded near the finish line of the Boston Marathon, killing three people and injuring 170 others, and the pursuit of the perpetrators ended four days later, with one of them killed and the other captured. Besides the official investigation led by law enforcement officials, there was a 'parallel investigation conducted by a growing movement of online sleuths, often referred to as cyber-vigilantes, or "digilantes". These groups, organically formed in ad hoc fashion, harness the power of collective knowledge and resources – "crowdsourcing" – towards a common purpose. In the Boston Marathon case, cyber-sleuths were pooling information and resources in order to assist the police in their criminal investigation of the bombing' (Nhan et al. 2015).

Nearly 12 years after the London Tube bombing and four years after the Boston Marathon US bombing, in Manchester, England, a 28 May 2017 suicide bombing at a large pop concert killed 22 people and injured dozens more. Within hours the police urged those who might have 'photos or video from their smartphones or dashcams to upload them to a dedicated server set up by the national U.K. authorities at ukpoliceimageappeal.co.uk'.[42]

Possibly the most interesting and pioneering, non-crime related examples of crowdsourcing was in 2009 when the *Guardian* created its pioneering, searchable online database with thousands of spending receipts of the Members of the British Parliament and asked the public to 'help mine the dataset for interesting information… Over 20,000 volunteers searched more than 170,000 documents, setting a new standard for the potential

[41] '7 July London Bombings: What Happened That Day?', BBC, 3 July 2015. http://www.bbc.com/news/uk-33253598. Lee Sangbok, 'The Impact of Video UGC Expansion on Participating Journalism', dissertation for MA in Global Media, University of Westminster, London, 2007, cited in de Burgh et al. 2008: 6.

[42] Seth Augenstein, 'Manchester Suicide Bombing: UK Police are Crowdsourcing, Investigating Terror Ties', *Forensic Magazine*, May 2017. https://www.forensicmag.com/news/2017/05/manchester-suicide-bombing-uk-police-are-crowdsourcing-investigating-terror-ties. Nazia Parveen, Frances Parraudin, and Vikram Dodd, *Guardian*, 28 May 2017. https://www.theguardian.com/uk-news/2017/may/28/armed-police-raid-moss-side-report-of-explosion.

of crowdsourced journalism to produce high audience engagement and tangible journalistic outcomes' (Onuoha 2015).

As Alan Rusbridger, the Editor-in-Chief of the *Guardian* for 20 years from 1995 to 2015, explained the phenomenon and importance of news organisations directly consulting their readers about various important issues of the day:

> *Would it be better as a newspaper to have as many other views as possible, and the answer is always yes. It has to be true. So, well, that's it, that's open journalism… Everywhere we tried it [crowdsourcing], it turned out to be true. We did it in sports, we did it in war reporting, we did it in education, [in] science, the environment. It was always true.*[43]

Among US news organisations, no one is more involved with gathering crowdsourced information for its reporting than ProPublica, the non-profit news organisation based in New York which has won four Pulitzer Prizes for its reporting since it began operation in 2008.[44] And no other American news organisation 'has cultivated the art of crowdsourcing like ProPublica. With patience and acumen, it has both embraced a unique mindset and developed a robust toolkit to transform enterprise journalism', according to a Columbia University Tow Center for Digital Journalism report. Its crowdsourcing has enriched several ProPublica exposés 'focusing on patient safety, nursing home inspections', surgeons, etc. (Onuoha 2015).

But no publisher in the world utilises the combined energies and wisdom of the crowd more broadly or extensively than Wikipedia, the self-described 'free online encyclopedia' founded by Jimmy Wales and Larry Sanger in 2001 and owned by the non-profit, US-based organisation Wikimedia Foundation. Not only is it 'the largest and most popular general reference work on the Internet', it is 'ranked among the ten most popular websites' in the world.[45] According to Wales, 70,000 to 80,000 people around the world edit Wikipedia at least five times a month, and within that, there is a smaller group of approximately 3,000–5,000 'core editors'.[46]

Another important development in the annals of the 21st-century

---

[43] Interview with Alan Rusbridger at Lady Margaret Hall College, University of Oxford, 30 Nov. 2015. Besides his role now as Principal of the College, he also now serves as Chair of the Reuters Institute for the Study of Journalism Steering Committee.

[44] https://www.propublica.org/about

[45] 'Wikipedia', https://en.wikipedia.org/wiki/Wikipedia. Lih 2009.

[46] Interview with Jimmy Wales, co-founder of Wikipedia, London, 4 Dec. 2015. See also Rusbridger 2009.

journalistic progress has been the creation of The Conversation, an independent, not-for-profit media outlet that primarily publishes information from the academic and research communities. It was launched in Australia in 2011 and in the UK in 2013, co-founded by Jack Rejtman (formerly with Yahoo News) and veteran British and Australian newspaper editor Andrew Jaspan, who was the Editor and Executive Director of The Conversation for six years, from 2011 to 2017. During that time, he 'secured funding and led the launches of the UK, US, Africa, French and Global editions'. As of April 2017, The Conversation worldwide has published '58,700 articles contributed by 26,000 scholars and researchers and scientists from 1,990 universities and research universities around the world'.[47]

The Conversation is the first entrepreneurial attempt to develop and publish editorial content written by thousands of academic and research scholars around the world, and also derive substantial operating revenue from financial contributions from colleges and universities.

In the US, at the American University (AU) School of Communication, I have informally proposed the creation of a new multidisciplinary academic field called Accountability Studies that 'would involve professors with different types of accountability knowledge and expertise from throughout the university' (Lewis 2014: 66–7). I am also a member of ECOllaborative, an informal network of AU professors across six schools interested in environmental-related policy and other issues. And, separately, in 2015, the non-profit news organisation I lead, the Investigative Reporting Workshop (which co-publishes/co-produces with the *Washington Post* and the PBS documentary programme Frontline), collaborated with a public anthropologist member of the AU Faculty, Associate Professor David Vine, assisting him with the graphics design and global mapping work relating to his book, and publishing an excerpt from it about the astonishing number and extent of US military bases and installations throughout the world.

All of this is positive and productive in terms of 'the possible' eclectic, research collaborations and the increasing needs to 'tear down' the various walls impeding their evolution and progress.

Fundamentally, for citizens of the world, the extraordinary reading, writing, and publishing possibilities and opportunities online are without precedent in history. There is a greater collective clamouring for information, for truth, for accountability now than at any previous time

---

[47] Misha Ketchell, 'Andrew Jaspan Resigns as Editor and Executive Director of The Conversation' (blog), 2 Apr. 2017. https://theconversation.com/andrew-jaspan-resigns-as-editor-and-executive-director-of-the-conversation-75600.

in history. And thanks to the internet and the World Wide Web and the ever-evolving global search engines and other recent computer-related capabilities, infinitely more information is also now readily available to us, and that will keep increasing exponentially. Now, we find ourselves in a previously unfathomable, symbiotic moment, a wholly new dimension in terms of professional, scholarly, technological, and creative communication and cooperation.

Imagine a world in which non-government organisation researchers, public interest activists, lawyers, government prosecutors and investigators, corporate investigators, forensic accountants, political scientists, computer and other scientists, investigative historians, public anthropologists, and journalists are occasionally looking in all the same places. Imagine that, to varying degrees, they are all beginning to utilise the same exciting new data technologies and analytics and other intellectual cross-pollination possibilities, exchanging ideas and sometimes working and writing together, side by side, across borders, genres.

These are collaborative, 21st-century fact-finders, fact-checkers, and more broadly, truth-travellers and truth tellers, searching for information, its verification and 'the truth', each of them coming from very different perspectives, education backgrounds, interests, professional expertise, not to mention internationally and culturally diverse geographic and economic circumstances. But despite these differences, they have much in common – they are all intrinsically curious and have an inordinate amount of patience, determination, and mettle. They are willing, if necessary, to persevere in their quest for answers for months, years, and sometimes even decades.

I find this suddenly noticeable, global community of interest in verifiable knowledge and understanding to be very exciting and auspicious, when it comes to the future of truth and, more narrowly, the future of journalism. For it is in our common interest, as citizens living in a representational democracy predicated on the principle of self-determination and self-government, to be reasonably well informed and to be able to distinguish between reality and unreality, fact from fiction and faction. We therefore *all* necessarily have a shared value in needing to know the basic truth of the matter, whatever that specific matter is. As Bill Kovach and Tom Rosenstiel noted in their seminal book, *The Elements of Journalism*, 'Journalism's first obligation is to the truth.' But as they also note, 'that, in turn, implies a two-way process. The citizen has an obligation to approach the news with an open mind and not just a desire that the news reinforce existing opinion' (Kovach and Rosenstiel 2007: 36–50, 249). As citizens, fundamentally, we *all* have an obligation to the truth. And I have never believed that the search for truth is, can be, or should be the exclusive preserve of journalists.

Facing the Future: Beyond the Current Conventions of Communication

All of the above explorations and initiatives regarding journalistic and other creative collaborations are important, constructive, and connote forward progress. But it is not unreasonable to also ask an inconvenient question. Are they sufficiently responsive to the serious, profound issues confronting this troubled world and, in particular, its pressing information and public accountability needs?

In this 'World Wide Web' era with its shared information, increasing collaboration, 'wisdom of the crowd' sensibilities, and also vast social networks in the millions of people, broadly interested in the same subjects or thematic, cross-border transcendent issues (e.g. health, environment, human rights, security, etc.), 21st-century newsgathering *must* rise above traditional but ultimately parochial metropolitan and nation-state geographic boundaries. The aperture of journalists' and citizens' lens must necessarily become much, much wider, outside borders, geographical and otherwise. Accountability of those in public and private power can and must continue to be precise and granular, of course, informed by specific, publicly available, accountability-related data. But it is the view of this author that the overall concept of public accountability – and, in particular, the important journalism about it – increasingly cannot and should not be narrowly confined by mere geographic boundaries, whether a town, city, county, state, or country.

Instead, it must consist more of broader, amassed knowledge and understanding, across borders, professional disciplines, and cultures, perhaps through the precise prism of documented, reliably sourced, public accountability issues in the world, in the context of the uses, the occasionally glaring, wilful non-uses, misuses, and abuses of political, corporate, and other power in the world. Imagine if you could combine the most authoritative, known information from various disparate sectors, including journalism, but also such academic areas of expertise such as investigative history, forensic accounting, computer science and statistics, political science, economics, public anthropology, human rights, public interest, and other law-related fields?

That kind of collaborative, accountability journalism, across fields, sectors, borders, and cultures, is all quite possible but it is still insufficiently explored because of various professional, political, logistical, and other encumbrances and realities.

The need to more fully illuminate the uses and abuses of power is quite obvious. Imagine a place online where you could go to find amassed, online searchable, accountability-related, primary documents-based information in the world from national and multilateral government offices that is credible, documented, and authoritative. Information, for example, about who *exactly* the worst corporate, financial scofflaws are, who the documented (based on government or criminal/civil court information) *worst* corporate violators of national or international safety, environmental, health, financial, and other laws and regulations are. Imagine a central, public registry online for all of the companies in the past decade decertified by one or more of the world's stock exchanges for fraud or other misbehaviour, all of the private interests found to have violated national and international laws worldwide, etc.

In terms of transparency, accountability, and responsive journalism and democracy, all of these things ideally should be available and accessible to the public today. But they aren't and it is probably quite unlikely that will change anytime soon.

But perhaps, as the 18th-century English writer Samuel Johnson reportedly found in a different context, we will unexpectedly encounter 'the triumph of hope over experience'.[48]

---

[48] From Fred R. Shapiro (ed.), *The Yale Book of Quotations* (New Haven: Yale University Press, 2006), 403.

2

The Elements of Collaboration

Richard Sambrook

Collaboration is never going to be straightforward within a journalism tradition which prides itself on exclusivity. To manage both the investigation and publication of a story in a way which preserves confidentiality, meets different cultural and publishing needs, and manages the legal, technical, and other requirements across multiple organisations and jurisdictions is necessarily complicated. It is understandable, then, that many of the biggest collaborative exercises have had a neutral intermediary or 'host' organisation helping to manage the collaboration – notably the ICIJ with the Panama and Paradise Papers, perhaps the most complex investigative collaborations to date.

In December 2016 the Reuters Institute for the Study of Journalism at Oxford University convened a workshop on collaboration in investigative journalism (see Appendix for list of participants). This full day of discussion explored the factors which help facilitate successful collaborative investigations – and those which hinder it. The workshop was followed by a debate at the 2017 International Journalism Festival in Perugia[49] and a small number of follow-up interviews. These discussions identified a number of factors discussed here.

Collaboration begs the question of who news organisations collaborate with. The idea of public collaboration – citizen journalism – as referred to in the last chapter by Charles Lewis, has been much analysed elsewhere and is outside the scope of this study. Crowdsourcing as a means of funding investigative journalism is a further type of public collaboration. However, we are focusing on editorial collaboration between professional news organisations, with NGOs of various kinds, with academia and other public bodies where it has delivered editorial value and opened up stories and issues which might otherwise have gone unreported.

---

[49] http://media.journalismfestival.com/programme/2017/investigating-big-data-collaboration-and-best-practise

We live in a time where there is more information openly available than ever – and an even greater quantity of data held confidentially. The nature of data and the internet, coupled with the impact of globalisation, means many organisations work internationally – and the issues that may arise from that are pan-national as well. Technology now allows the gathering, analysis, and sharing of data in unprecedented ways.

Consequently, as one workshop participant put it, 'the challenge is to get reporters around the world to share information they have that they may not wish to share. Stories now begin in one country and end up on the other side of the world so we need to work out some way of pooling this information without cutting across our own editorial needs.'[50]

Trust

Building trust between potential partners is therefore essential. Those involved in major collaborations are clear that the crucial issue is simply how well you know and trust those you are working alongside. There have been some cases of non-disclosure or other agreements being introduced in advance – but that appears to be the exception. In the big investigations to date, it has largely been a question of mutual trust, often simply founded on a newsroom handshake. As one journalist put it, 'you cannot codify relationships'.

Having said that, there have been written agreements in place to manage publication schedules, for example. As one ICIJ member recalls:

> We have partnered on projects where every reporter needs to sign an agreement and the agreement is a very simple agreement that states you're going to credit ICIJ, and you're to cite any mistakes, and we're all going to publish together, and ICIJ has the final word on what we publish together. I think that that has been a point of discussion, for example, in our conversations with US partners because some US partners did not like that fact that we would get to say when the investigation was going to be published, but it's the only way. Like somebody has to have this neutral position ... because we realised that if we published everything all together around the world on one day, it would be have far greater impact.[51]

---

[50] RISJ Workshop, 16 Dec. 2016 (discussion was under Chatham House rules – allowing quotes without attribution).
[51] Ibid.

This usually works when the partners are not directly competing – newspapers and broadcasters, or organisations working in different languages or with non-competing readers or audiences in different countries. In the Panama Papers, the ICIJ saw a large part of its role as nurturing and managing partnerships in a non-competitive way – acting as trusted intermediary.

Some involved believe relationships are built from the newsroom up, not from the senior executive suite. 'It is interesting to think about the structures within organisations and which bits of organisations collaborate', said one workshop participant.

> *Journalists have always been quite good at collaborating because they have always collaborated with their sources, with politicians, with academics and have usually worked with more than one person on their stories. But when it comes to editors, and lawyers, they're actually quite difficult at collaborating, they want to own the story.*[52]

Perhaps unsurprisingly, executives disagree. Javier Moreno of *El País*, responding to the suggestion that editors are less interested in collaborations, put it like this:

> *Publishers have a very clear idea of what they want to reach and they see clearly the benefits of bringing 27 newspapers, which are not competitors, together. Publishers see the long term benefit for these alliances – if you are in the newsroom, fighting for every square inch of paper you have a different perspective.*[53]

Collaborations inevitably bring tensions. As Stefan Candea of the European Investigative Collaborations Network wrote about the football leaks story on the EIC blog:

> *To have so many different journalists working together for so many months on a secret data-set can't happen without discovering big differences. Sometimes this has led to tensions and heated discussions and open criticism … we knew most of the tensions will be related to the publication schedule. This part involved a lot of discussions and compromises on all sides, since everybody wants to host the stories exclusively. It was a lot of time and energy put into this to satisfy the logistical questions of print*

---

[52] Ibid.
[53] Ibid.

deadlines of weeklies that appear on different days or of online publications that have diverse rules on paywall or no paywall.[54]

Alan Rusbridger, Editor of the *Guardian* during the Wikileaks Iraq files story, agrees:

It was logistically horrible trying to collaborate with a German weekly, a French afternoon paper, a New York morning paper and so on, trying to get the logistics right. But it was a really valuable learning experience. We learned from the New York Times and from Der Spiegel. It established a network of people who knew each other.[55]

Different legal environments and editorial standards can impact how organisations work together. Alan Rusbridger recalls taking the Snowden revelations to US news organisations. He believed a clear focus on Snowden, the NSA, and GCHQ was essential to defending publication in the UK. But American partners did not understand why a British newspaper would want to redact some parts of the intelligence.

They had people saying, 'Well, we're interested in the Kenyan, Nairobi massacre, at the shopping mall', and they found really good stuff there. I said, 'No, I'm sorry that's not the agreement and I can't. If you publish that they (British security services) will come at me and say, "That's got nothing to do with Snowden … you're just trawling through (any) British intelligence to do with a terrorist attack" and the Americans pushed back and said, 'Well it's obviously public. We wouldn't think twice about running these stories.'[56]

For these reasons, as Brigitte Alfter explores in the next chapter, successful collaborations often depend on a 'neutral' editorial coordinator who can resolve some of these tensions. It's a new emerging role, but one which calls on the traditional strengths of a news editor or editorial manager in running a complex operation. They can also help to mediate some of the cultural differences. For example, America has a much stronger fact-checking tradition – which can seem pedantic to others. The British are keener on secret filming than other countries, the Germans have another approach again. David Alandete, the Managing Editor of *El País*, put it like this:

[54] https://eic.network/blog/making-a-network
[55] Interview with author, Apr. 2017.
[56] RISJ Workshop, 16 Dec. 2016.

Germans are very fact based. They use a lot of quotes. I guess the Spanish press uses fewer quotes and shorter quotes. I think you have to adapt the style to your reader and for that you have to consider that you cannot just translate a German story into Spanish. You need to modify it, to adapt it for your reader. I know this very well because we have several editions. We operate not only in Spain but also in Latin America and Brazil in Portuguese. And we have to [make] this effort of translating our own content even if it's in the same language. We have to adapt to Mexico or Argentina so you have to approach the reader with a language and a style that he or she will feel comfortable with. And that is always going to be the biggest problem.[57]

Under the pressure of a long-running complex investigation these different practices can become problematic unless there is a structure and process in place to manage them.

Equally there are differences in approach between print and TV. These differences can also impinge on production and publication times. As one interviewee, Frederik Obermaier, who was at the heart of the Panama Papers investigation, commented:

It started with differences between TV media and print media. The TV guys of course have a longer cycle of production so they need more time than print production. I write an article, look for a photo and create a good layout – you can do that within hours. But producing a 30-minute documentary takes lots of time. Even if you have all the A roll and B roll you still have to cut it … We had another issue, in Germany the best day for a newspaper is Friday or Saturday. But we soon realised that in other countries the weekend is a bad time to publish – there's nobody reading them on a Saturday, or TV may not have a suitable programme scheduled then. In the end we agreed on a Sunday evening which was when most partners could go.[58]

Negotiating these conflicts of interest requires high levels of trust to be developed – and trust, in turn, relies on well-established confidentiality.

---

[57] Interview with author, Apr. 2017.
[58] Interview with author, Apr. 2017.

Confidentiality

For the Panama Papers, some 400 journalists were working on the material for a year – but remarkably nothing leaked. As one ICIJ team member put it:

> Yes, of course we had concerns because I mean it is a matter of fact that journalists are chatty people especially after one or two beers we all tend ... to speak to our friends about what we are currently doing and so there was a huge risk of this story being leaked before the agreed date of publication. If you think about 400 journalists and each of them are only telling one person then you are already speaking about 800 people all around the world knowing about this project. And then bosses had to be involved, lawyers that had to be involved. So for me it is still a miracle that nothing big leaked before the publication, and it showed me that all members of this team realised how important it is to stick to the rules and to not reveal anything before the date which we agreed on all together.[59]

Of course for the journalists involved it may well be the biggest story of their careers with their professional integrity on the line, so the incentives to respect the collaboration and confidentiality are – professionally – high. The scale and importance of the story – and the fact it may only be reportable through collaboration – provide key incentives, as Alan Rusbridger notes:

> It's very difficult. I think that's where you need to build up the trust element in the collaboration ... You cannot go into collaboration without trusting everybody in the collaboration because they're all going to tell their boyfriend, their girlfriend, their next door neighbour, their best friend. And so you've got to make sure that there's enough incentive that they don't break the big story before anyone else.[60]

Consequently, breakdowns in trust and confidentiality can have lasting effects. The differences between Wikileaks and their media partners over redaction of material has meant their initial partners are no longer prepared to work with Julian Assange and his team and, as a consequence, their impact has declined (see Beckett and Ball 2010).

---

[59] RISJ Workshop, 16 Dec. 2016.
[60] RISJ Workshop, 16 Dec. 2016.

Scale and Resources

Clearly a major motivation for collaborating is pooling resources and expertise to decipher unfamiliar documents or data or to cope with the scale of a leak. Alan Rusbridger recalls the scale of the data leaked by Edward Snowden:

> *I don't know how many documents we had, but let's say hundreds of thousands. Every one of them was completely unfamiliar. It was just filled with acronyms and stuff, and we didn't really have a national security reporter in the way that America does, so we were starting from complete scratch. Really good reporters like David Leigh and Nick Davies (both Guardian investigative reporters) who were as good as anyone in the world, they were just staring at these documents ... but the New York Times had people who had done this and nothing else. And ProPublica did too. So it made sense to go to them. The second issue was technological. We had James Ball (a data journalist now with BuzzFeed) who understood the technology, but trying to get people who understood how the internet was wired and worked and how encryption worked, we just didn't have that in-house apart from James.*[61]

Frederik Obermaier of the German newspaper *Süddeutsche Zeitung* has a similar view about handling the Panama Papers data leak:

> *We realised that the amount of data was by far too big. Secondly we soon realised that there are so many leads in the data to other countries and scandals that might not be too relevant for a German audience. But, for example, to an audience in Angola, in Russia, in Azerbaijan they would be relevant. So we thought that it would be a pity not to research these parts of the data only because the audience of Süddeutsche Zeitung may not be interested. So we decided to share the material with the ICIJ and that's with more than 400 journalists all around the world.*[62]

---

[61] RISJ Workshop, 16 Dec. 2016.
[62] Interview with author, Apr. 2017.

Intermediaries and Networks

As organisations seek to share material and pool expertise and resources, the cultural and operational problems come into play. For this reason, 'neutral' intermediaries like the ICIJ prove valuable – particularly when they can also bring technology expertise. Mar Cabra of ICIJ recalls how they were brought into the Panama Papers by *Süddeutsche Zeitung*:

> *Most of what we do is project management plus the technology services. When Bastian Obermayer (of* Süddeutsche Zeitung*) came to us he said they didn't know what to do with so much data ... but it's lots of work. A collaboration doesn't necessarily make your life easy. A lot of the work we do is like being the coach of a team where we're saying 'yeah come on guys, pass the ball!' It requires incentives. Collaboration is a tool, just like competition is a tool, so when you select partners ... you use the competition to strengthen the incentive.*[63]

The right mix of commercial and non-profit media is also a factor. Big media organisations can provide the platform and exposure that non-profit media need. The non-profits bring access to data and highly developed expertise which the major media companies may not have in-house. This is the model for a new data journalism initiative from the Bureau for Investigative Journalism in London.

It hired Megan Lucero from *The Times* to lead the team which will work with local media to provide local investigative, data-led stories which they would be unable to find or process themselves. She explains:

> *It's a truly collaborative environment. In the sense that we are not just providing a data wire or a data service, and we're not handing people stories. We are collaborating together on those investigations, with the idea that no one person is better than the other. That local knowledge is just as valuable as tech experience.*[64]

The intention is to build a network of collaborating organisations, starting small and learning as they grow. The bureau will offer time, expertise, technology, and the local partners will offer the platform and local knowledge:

[63] RISJ Workshop, 16 Dec. 2016.
[64] Interview with author, Apr. 2017.

Maybe it's something that would take a whole sequence database that needs clearing, or maybe it needs a series of matching, or matching data-sets or putting multiple things together. We would do that heavy lifting, and part of that will be informed by what the various people in our network find really interesting about that story, and what would want to query in that story and that will help inform it. And as we're going, we're very open about what we're doing, and everyone's contributing, and then we have an embargo on it, and allows local journalists to dig into that and find their story angles. And they'll need to share what they're finding with everyone else in the network; we all benefit from that. And then the idea tends to be that we all break together according to the embargo date.

This kind of network of non-competing local outlets, with a non-profit intermediary bringing expertise and resources, embodies the new approach to delivering investigative journalism that would not otherwise be reported.

Finance

The importance of non-profit journalism organisations to these large-scale collaborations begs the question of finance. In the US there are well-established foundations and a culture of philanthropy which has traditionally supported non-profit journalism, from National Public Radio to ProPublica, the Center for Public Integrity, and the ICIJ. Increasingly the big technology companies are seeking to improve their relationships with news providers through grants – such as Google's Digital News Initiative. But generally in Europe, and other parts of the world, the culture of philanthropy is less well developed and finding sustainable funding for non-profit journalism is significantly harder as a consequence.

This in itself is one reason non-profit organisations like the Bureau for Investigative Journalism are driven to collaborate with major organisations – to find distribution and profile for their journalism but also to supplement their operation with the resources (and journalism) others can bring to the project.

The Bureau discovered that traditional commissioning budgets (as offered, for example, to independent TV production companies) weren't sufficient to cover both the cost of undertaking the journalism and the TV production. Trying to work commercially did not deliver a sustainable income to manage the core costs of expensive, long-running investigations. So they moved to third-party funding – which in turn raises the issue of what the funders – be it foundations or NGOs – expect in return for their investment.

Rachel Oldroyd, the Bureau's Managing Editor, said:

There is a lot of funding out there for doing stories on certain things, but if you have an agenda then it's unlikely to get the media partners involved because they will say 'well, who is paying for this story?' … So it has to be general support (core) funding only and you have to find funders that basically just want to see social change in a broad sense.[65]

The Bureau has diversified its range of supporters and funders in order to ensure no one organisation can be seen to wield decisive editorial influence over its journalism.

This poses questions about editorial independence from funders and where a line is drawn between a legitimate alignment of interests in an investigation and potentially steering an agenda in a way which compromises editorial independence. In today's more activist media environment – where traditional objectivity and impartiality are less highly valued – does such an agenda matter if the funding relationship is transparent? (These questions are explored in more detail by Anne Koch in Chapter 5 in relation to NGOs and journalism.)

The Bill and Melinda Gates Foundation funded a Global Development website with the *Guardian* in 2010 to 'hold governments, institutions and NGOs accountable for the implementation of the United Nations millennium development goals'. Public accountability for delivery of explicit commitments is obviously an area of legitimate journalistic interest as well as, in this case, a core objective of the Foundation. As Alan Rusbridger, Editor of the *Guardian* at the time, put it:

It is essential to have a place where some of the biggest questions facing humanity are analysed and debated, and through which we can monitor the effectiveness of the billions of pounds of aid that flows annually into the developing world.

Conflicts can, of course, arise. He later reflected that the only stipulation was that the *Guardian* had to write about the millennium development goals. 'We were free to criticise Gates … there were no conditions put on the grant.'[66]

---

[65] RISJ Workshop, 16 Dec. 2016.
[66] Interview with author, Apr. 2017.

Greenpeace is an NGO which has decided to invest in investigative journalism. The charity funds an investigative team, which work independently of the rest of the charity, and offer stories to the media as well as publishing on their own site. 'Investigative journalism is the new direct action', as one member explained.[67] For Greenpeace, it ensures accountability journalism is conducted on issues at the heart of their mission – in this case sustainable energy. They have placed items – for free – in many national newspapers, but admit it is harder to work with regulated broadcasters, like the BBC, or papers committed to objectivity, like the *New York Times*.

For organisations collaborating with NGOs or funders, agreement about success and metrics in advance is important. What is success? Many of the metrics remain loose or intangible. Measuring qualities like impact or engagement remains an inexact science – although many are trying to develop new indicators. But unless all partners are agreed on what they are seeking to achieve and how they will judge if they have done so, collaborations may be difficult or short term.

The American academic James T. Hamilton has demonstrated that a single dollar invested in journalism can generate hundreds of dollars in social benefits (Hamilton 2016). But this is not yet a widely accepted principle. Many NGOs and foundations still see the media as a tool to deliver other benefits (e.g. healthcare) rather than independent journalism being an objective in its own right – one which delivers further broad social and political benefits. As such, public funding for accountability journalism is unlikely to deliver a long-term sustainable model outside of the US. But collaboration between different partners, in different sectors of the media or the third sector, can help such funding as is available go further and deliver journalism and benefits which would otherwise be unachievable.

Technology

Collaborative investigations depend on a number of levels of technology. First, the scale of data released in a leak like that of Edward Snowden or the Panama Papers requires technology and technical expertise to hold and analyse.

Then there is technology required to maintain confidentiality – through encryption or other techniques. There may be defensive technology required to prevent external (or internal) hacking of databases, emails,

---

[67] Interview with author, Apr. 2017.

or other communications. And for global collaborations, there is a need for technology to manage the partnership, sharing material and working jointly on data from different locations.

The scale of data handling required from a major leak is outside the competence of most news organisations. As Mar Cabra of ICIJ explained about their role in the Panama Papers:

> *Süddeutsche Zeitung came to us with 2.6 terabytes of data – equivalent to 11.5 million documents. And one of the things we did was to get software built for other purposes to help manage it and make it searchable. So, for example, software built for searching books in libraries and repurposing it for journalism. We repurposed a social networking tool used for dating to support collaboration of investigative journalists.*[68]

Süddeutsche Zeitung explained how they analysed the Paradise Papers alongside publication:

> *The Paradise Papers consist of dozens of different data formats, including emails, PDFs, text documents, images and information from databases. To make sense of this tangle of data, Süddeutsche Zeitung used the software Nuix, a program also used by international investigative authorities. The same program was used to evaluate the Panama Papers. The program makes it possible to easily search through all of the datasets and compare the data with lists of important people and companies. In addition, ICIJ made the data available to all of the media partners involved in the reporting on a platform programmed specifically for this project. That allowed journalists across the globe to work on the material around the clock.*[69]

A quarter of ICIJ staff are now developers rather than journalists. Using open-source software, which can be repurposed and built upon was key – as well as avoiding major software manufacturers' proprietary code or use-tracking.

Encryption is now assumed as standard for major investigations – including use of Virtual Private Networks, Tor browser (although increasingly there are doubts whether that remains secure), encrypted messaging applications, and PGP-encrypted emails. However, a number of journalists pointed out that by the time a whistleblower has approached

---

[68] RISJ workshop, 16 Dec. 2016.
[69] https://projekte.sueddeutsche.de/paradisepapers/wirtschaft/answers-to-pressing-questions-about-the-leak-e574659/ (Accessed 7th November 2017)

a journalist it might be too late to protect their identity. If they have used non-encrypted messaging, or a mobile phone, they will be traceable.

The Snowden NSA revelations have made it clear that nothing is secure unless it is encrypted from beginning to end or avoids any contact with the internet. Paper may be the most secure technology of all.

Defensive technology can extend to monitoring incoming traffic to see if anyone is trying to access a network – not something that all smaller organisations can afford, although some software companies will provide technology for free out of corporate responsibility or in return for being associated with a high-profile investigation.

The stronger awareness of these security issues in some investigative teams may be a benefit for newsrooms which have not yet had to confront them. But equally, the lack of awareness of even basic security is a risk for partnerships.

Casual email conversation between partners could jeopardise a story – not only if it is intercepted. In any subsequent legal challenge the disclosure of casual comments about the story could undermine its standing. There are different legal provisions in relation to disclosure in libel and defamation proceedings between countries. Many journalists don't realise how incautious emails can come back to haunt them in a court case under legal discovery. Communication hygiene is both a technology issue and a cultural and practice issue – but one which has mixed understanding in most newsrooms.

Collaborations can also bring greater awareness of publicly available software and verification techniques which some newsrooms may not yet have adopted.

As Eliot Higgins of the Bellingcat site said:

> There's an education issue. A lot of organisations don't have a clue about things like location and the basics of verifying video or a photograph. You can use Google Analytics IDs to link lots of different websites or investigate troll factories. There's a search engine that can do that for you, but hardly anyone knows that's even a thing that's possible to do. Not everyone needs that skill, but they should know it's possible.[70]

Offering training programmes can become an important activity for non-profit specialist organisations like the ICIJ or the UK's Centre for Investigative Journalism.

---

[70] RISJ Workshop, 16 Dec. 2016.

Technology expertise is a crucial component of collaborations. As Frederik Obermaier of *Süddeutsche Zeitung* explained:

> *Without the platforms ICIJ provided, this project (Panama Papers) would have been impossible. From our side, as the one media organisation contributing data, it was very important not to – for example – send hard disks with all the data around the world and lose control of it. So the platform ICIJ set up where all partners could in a safe and secure manner and encrypted way access the data gave us a better feeling about security. It also allowed ICIJ to monitor who was accessing what across the network. Having a collaboration space ... was a really crucial part of the investigation.*[71]

Case Study

The Football Leaks

A good example of the importance of technology to pan-national collaborative investigations is set out by the EIC in a blog post about the Football Leaks – the largest leak in the history of sports.

The post outlines how the EIC set up an Apple laptop to process the data, using a self-developed tool, 'Snoop'. They placed the data on a secure HTTPS website for the 12 contributing news organisations to access, using two-step authentication for security. They then used another software product to extract text and metadata from a group of different file format documents and emails. More software combinations were used to attach metadata from the text to each document, ready for journalists to search. Communication between partners was through an open-source clone of the Slack application. The group has made the source code for their developed software freely available on GitHub under the name 'hoover' for the umbrella project. It's a strong example of how technology development needs to work closely with journalists to be able to process, index, search, and communicate about a large quantity of leaked data between collaborating partners in different organisations and different countries.[72]

---

[71] RISJ Workshop, 16 Dec. 2016.
[72] https://eic.network/blog/how-to-investigate-football-leaks

Conclusions

The discussions at the Reuters Institute workshop and International Journalism Festival panel debate highlighted a number of key factors lying behind successful collaborations. These factors need to be considered in advance and actively managed by any groups planning cross-national collaborations to heighten the chances of success. They include:

- Trust building between different organisations, usually from a newsroom level upwards, initially. Newsroom staff find the benefits of collaboration easier to identify than senior executives, who may be overly focused on exclusivity or other competitive factors.
- Confidentiality is crucial and needs to be supported by a high level of 'communication hygiene'. By the time a whistleblower has contacted a news organisation their identity may already be compromised. Secure channels of communication – such as 'dropboxes' – need to be set up and publicised.
- If non-profit organisations are involved, or third-party funders, objectives and success measures need to be agreed in advance together with principles of editorial independence.
- Technology, and the ability to develop and modify software or other technology to suit the needs of a particular project, is crucial. Developers and journalists need to work in an integrated way.
- A neutral partner – such as a non-profit news organisation or jointly owned joint venture – can play a valuable role in managing tensions and potential conflicts of interest between partners. In the end, one trusted party has to make decisions and hold other partners to account.

In the next chapter, Brigitte Alfter of Journalismfund.eu explores some of these issues in more depth through interviews and cross-border case studies and in particular identifies the importance of – and key characteristics for – the new role of editorial coordinator.

3

New Method, New Skill, New Position? Editorial Coordinators in Cross-Border Collaborative Teams

Brigitte Alfter

The focus of this chapter is on the work process of practitioners in the field of collaborative journalism. The aim is to contribute to an understanding of *editorial coordination* and the role, function, and skills of editorial coordinators – a specialised role which is increasingly required to manage cross-border collaborations (as identified in the last chapter). An understanding of these processes can be applied not only by cross-border collaborative journalism groups but also other collaborative teams where one of the partners is a journalist or for any medium that needs to observe legal rules, ethical guidelines, communication with target groups, as well as respect editorial independence to obtain credibility.

Definitions and Questions

For this chapter, the process-oriented definition of cross-border journalism includes four features:

(1) Journalists from different countries, who …
(2) cooperate on a shared theme or story, they …
(3) compile, mutually cross-check and ultimately merge their findings to …
(4) individually fact-check and publish these findings adjusted to their national, local or otherwise specialised target groups (Alfter 2016).

This definition can be adapted to other collaborative journalism efforts in that the first feature of 'journalists from different countries' can be replaced by any cooperating team of disparate character such as journalists and scholars, for example.

Though not explicitly mentioned, the process-oriented definition corresponds with Reese, who defines 'a practice of "global" journalism' as one that is 'carried out in such a way that the producers, users, and subjects need not, and often do not, share a common national orientation' (Reese 2007: 40).

Peter Berglez demands a 'global outlook' (Berglez 2008), perceiving that the media and journalists do not fulfil their role as 'global fourth estate' (Berglez 2013). Coming from an analysis of science journalism and knowledge sharing within societies, scholars like the Danish team of researchers Meyer and Brink Lund attempt to carve out the influence on journalism and indeed society of the underlying frameworks of thought in different language areas (Meyer and Brink Lund 2008). This, similar to the thoughts of Reese, can be helpful for the practical work in collaborative journalism teams.

While building upon the developments in journalism and media research with its particular 'complexity and novelty of theorising global phenomena' (Reese 2007: 41), this chapter stays within the practical rather than theoretical realm. The hope is that it can gather and contextualise the experience of journalists and teams of journalists to understand the role of the individual journalist in a transnational team of journalists, the working of a cross-border journalism team or network, and the structures in such networks.

To gather such a description the following questions are addressed within the overall question of 'New method, new skill, new position?':

(1) Composing a cross-border journalism team
(2) Decision-making and how to structure a cross-border journalism network
(3) The role and tasks of the editorial coordinator
(4) Dealing with cultural/national/professional differences
(5) Perceived needed competences for coordination

Methodology

Six editorial coordinators from five cross-border journalism teams were interviewed in semi-structured interviews focusing on work process questions such as team composition, decision-making-structures, work routines, and so forth. Based upon the replies the responses then are structured in the above groups.

Throughout it has to be noted that the author should be considered a participant observer. Conducting cross-border research with my own initiated ad-hoc teams (since 2004 and actively in journalism until 2012) and with the ICIJ (member since 2008 and actively involved in journalism until 2012) provided practitioner insights and privileged access to ICIJ core team members. As managing editor of Journalismfund.eu I gained early insight into the planning and set-up of multiple ad-hoc European cross-border teams.

Interviews

Except for the ICIJ deputy editor the interviewees are predominantly European. This is not to exclude networks elsewhere, but to use the above-mentioned participant observer privilege of insight into the characteristics of available cross-border journalism projects.

The interviewees include appointed and full-time editorial coordinators as well as team members doing journalism themselves while also coordinating the team. Ad-hoc as well as more permanent structures were included, and the size of the teams coordinated was taken into consideration in the selection.

While larger and long-term teams such as the ICIJ network have gained experience and can analyse and describe the role, function, and tasks of editorial coordination, newly formed teams have expressed surprise at the challenge of coordination on top of the journalistic tasks. Diversity of experience in cross-border teams as well as size and structure thus was attempted in the selection of interviewees. Only teams who have already published their findings have been included.

The interviews were conducted by phone or face-to-face in the spring of 2017.

The Cases

The International Consortium of Investigative Journalists (ICIJ)

A permanent global network coordinated by a team of editors here represented by deputy editor-in-chief Marina Walker. The ICIJ was founded in 1997 as a project under the US-based non-profit journalism Centre for Public Integrity and spun off as an independent non-profit journalism structure in 2017. In the early years the ICIJ worked with a network of hand-picked, often award-winning or otherwise renowned investigative journalists. Since the Lux Leaks investigation in 2014 this structure was turned into a more general networking resource while the ICIJ now focuses on being a facilitator of large data-sets and networking assistance to media partners with individual journalists appointed at those media.

European Investigative Collaborations (EIC)

A permanent European network coordinated by Stefan Candea. Initiated in 2015 by German news magazine *Der Spiegel,* EIC involves established media, investigative journalism centres, and freelance journalists. First publications in 2016.

Investigate Europe

A European start-up network coordinated by Elisa Simantke. Prepared since 2015 and beginning work in 2016, the team of nine individual journalists from eight countries aims to become a permanent structure. Its team members are either connected to media outlets on a part-time basis or freelancers.

The 'Security for Sale' Team

An ad-hoc team coordinated by Maaike Goslinga, international editor at *De Correspondent,* Netherlands. *De Correspondent* aims to look at structural questions rather than day-to-day stories, and the task of the international editor is to find relevant collaborating journalists or media. 'I'm foreign desk 2.0', says Goslinga. For the Security for Sale research on public funding of the European security industry Maaike Goslinga coordinated a team of 22 journalists from European countries. The project was published in 2017.

The 'Migrants Files' Team

An ad-hoc team coordinated by Sylke Gruhnwald – then data desk editor at *Neue Zürcher Zeitung*, now with the start-up Republik.ch – and Nicolas Kayser-Bril of Journalism++. In the early stages the team consisted of eight journalists and grew slightly before the two publications in 2013 and 2014.

Findings

An experienced journalist once muttered 'cross-border journalism is not rocket science', and indeed, it is not. Cross-border journalism is a combination of good, journalism with all the aspects of its practice – from the day-to-day media newsroom to the large investigative journalism projects – with the necessary communication technology, insights into networking with colleagues and media in potentially very different situations, security considerations, and project management. The complexity of the transnational projects adds further requirements to their coordination.

All those interviewed expressed the need for coordination – hardly surprising given the selection of interviewees. However, this need surfaced also in ad-hoc or young teams, some of which had an initial ideal of a very flat and/or networked structure without a coordinator.

Here the findings of the interviews will be described grouped along the lines of the working questions described above.

Composing a Cross-Border Journalism Team

Composing a cross-border team is a delicate matter. A reliable and well-functioning team is crucial when working closely with colleagues and – sometimes – under pressure or with sensitive sources and material. All interviewees had thought carefully about the matter and composed teams according to the perceived needs – be that for ad-hoc research or a long-term vision.

In the following the teams will be introduced as interviewees describe the team-building process.

Gathering New Teams and Enlarging Established Teams

The challenge of team building in cross-border journalism teams could indicate the value of long-term collaborations in single groups and of long-term contacts with trusted individual colleagues. 'The ICIJ has the advantage to have composed these teams for many years. It's a big advantage to have an established network', says Marina Walker of the ICIJ. In the early years of its existence, the ICIJ composed a network of journalists, many of whom had been through US fellowships or otherwise marked themselves as visionaries. After about ten years of its existence the ICIJ started to invite younger generations, 'hungrier for the story and a great promise of journalism in their countries', as well as 'more ready to work in teams', says Walker. Trust is considered something that is built by working with a person for years. New investigations bring in new journalists and the network of trust is gradually expanded. In recent years the 'membership badge' has been toned down by the ICIJ, though Walker acknowledges that journalists 'still like to be called members, it helps in their careers, they consider it an honour, and sometimes they represent the ICIJ and speak well for the values of the organisation'. Before inviting a new team member the ICIJ does 'a little investigation' into the track record of a potential partner which includes references of their work, whether they are good team players, whether they're good at finding solutions and easy to communicate with. 'Not everybody has that profile, it's not a judgement as not everyone is for collaboration', says Walker, also mentioning invitees who declined membership as they preferred to continue working by themselves.

New partners are invited for new investigations to suit 'the need of the investigation' in terms – for example – of countries. Considerations about involving journalists from media organisations 'that are diverse enough to get really good coverage', such as platform diversity within a given country, are part of the criteria, says Walker about the ICIJ.

When Stefan Candea and German weekly news magazine *Der Spiegel* established European Investigative Collaborations, the EIC network, 'trust' was a key word to build the team. Initially a concept paper was developed by Candea on behalf of *Spiegel*, 'built around people of trust, not around media partners but trust in specific persons', says Candea. Himself a journalist well experienced in cross-border journalism, he brought such trusted contacts into the new network with a weight on colleagues with experience in cross-border journalism and their geographic location in Europe. Once a core group was established and a workflow prepared and agreed upon, further members were invited into the network according to the same criteria of trust and geography.

The Investigate Europe structure is set to be a new, permanent European network, 'a start-up', as coordinator Elisa Simantke puts it. The idea was conceived while reporting on the Euro-crisis in Germany, Greece, and Portugal in bi- or trilateral investigative projects by two German, a Greek, a Portuguese, and a Norwegian journalist. The ambition is to investigate essential European topics even if these are complex. Supported by foundation money, the team aims at developing a model for a permanent structure. Driven ahead by one journalist and the core group of early peers, the selection of team members was largely geographic and based upon commitment to the overall objective. Establishing trust and work routines was an important part of the first months at work.

In the ad-hoc Security for Sale project coordinated by *De Correspondent*, geography played a role. Based upon preliminary data analysis of the big security industry in Europe, Goslinga and her colleagues at *De Correspondent* found a number of Western European countries with large security industries. They added Italy due to the refugee situation there. Colleagues were selected based upon their previous writing about the security industry, then further data journalists were added to the team. Goslinga and her colleague selected partners as they had developed the idea and the initial data analysis. *De Correspondent* team explicitly attempted a balanced team with younger and senior members as well as a gender-balanced team, which in some cases proved to be a time-consuming challenge which required support from the editor at *De Correspondent*. The team embraced freelancers and media partners alike, and time was invested by *De Correspondent* to secure funding for the freelancers. 'I do not believe in collaboration with outlets only, you leave too many good freelancers out', says Goslinga.

Another ad-hoc team coordinated by Sylke Gruhnwald and Nicolas Kayser-Bril, the Migrants Files Project, set out to build a database of people who died during their attempt to reach Europe. The idea came from an Italian colleague. Informal networking contacts established during investigative and data journalism conferences in Europe provided the pool from which the team was selected. 'Conferences' infrastructure plays an important role to build teams. This is how you meet. It is also important to strengthen the network of the people you work with. The network is the entrance to such work', says Gruhnwald. Selection criteria included geography – where the team reached out to one per country to avoid competition – and interest in the field.

All interviewees mention that fluctuation in the teams was low, though it was important that team members were given time by their editors to work in the group.

Summing up, it is obvious that professional competence and geography are emphasised by all interviewees. Specialisation in a topic is a requirement particularly by the ad-hoc teams researching one topic but also European expertise by the Investigate Europe team working on multiple topics with a

European angle. A methodological experience with investigative or cross-border journalism is also among the competences mentioned by several interviewees. One coordinator mentioned team player personalities as a criterion, while another stipulated diversity in the team in gender and junior/senior experience. Two interviewees explicitly mentioned the need to include both staffers and freelancers in the team with the objective to involve the most competent and specialised colleagues. Trust in colleagues was emphasised widely, as was the value of the individuals' professional networks.

Team/Network Structures

The functioning of such teams obviously relies upon some of the factors identified for team selection.

Three of the teams were selected in what could be seen as a bottom-up manner: journalists have an idea for a research (Migrants Files, Security for Sale) or indeed a long-term structure (Investigate Europe) and select colleagues to make this plan happen. The role of the initiator or initiators is important at this moment. One team (ICIJ) had been launched 20 years ago and built its team selection on long-term experience and relationships. However, here too the selection criteria resembled the others.

The initiator – be that for a given topic or for the entire set-up – has been mentioned by most interviewees as having a special role, either because no team members are there yet, and the initiator sets up a team, or because the initiator within a given structure brings in an idea or data trove and has a special influence and position for that particular investigation.

Team Overlap

ICIJ has urged traditionally competing national media to cooperate on an investigation and simply set cooperation as a condition to get access to the data trove. The overall objective was to reach out to wider audiences by involving team members from different media platforms. Several interviewees of the ad-hoc teams mentioned that they avoided multiple team members from the same country to avoid competition. There was some overlap between some of the interviewed networks in that members of the EIC network as well as one member of the Security for Sale team also are members of the ICIJ. While national media often have a fierce internal competition, collaborative journalism so far has had a less competitive approach, using the advantages of selecting only one journalist or media partner per country. However, overlapping networks mean new frontiers of media competition may move into the journalism networks.

Decision-Making and How to Structure a Cross-Border Journalism Network

Decision-making is intrinsically linked with the structure and the size of a team or network. Key decisions on editorial material, publication dates, and team composition stand out. All teams worked with a coordinator. Also the initiator – or the one who 'owns' the journalistic idea or material – is mentioned by several teams as having a particular role when it comes to making decisions.

All the teams described in this chapter had the ambition to share all information with all team members. This is contrary to other examples where a data trove is held by one player and shared with selected media partners, for example for one nation or language area. Such models are not included in this chapter.

All teams describe an initial face-to-face meeting to prepare an investigation and make general decisions. The everyday work after that meeting differs between teams, with a noticeable difference between the three permanent and the two ad-hoc teams most obvious when it comes to meeting frequency. The ICIJ, EIC, and IE, for example, have weekly phone conferences, supplemented with a physical team meeting every three to four months.

Among the smaller teams, the need to coordinate and the workload connected came as a surprise. 'It emerged there was a need to coordinate', say Sylke Gruhnwald and Nicolas Kayser-Bril on their bottom-up experience with the Migrants Files Project. Only after getting started the role of the – in this case two – coordinators was described and handed to the two team members. The Investigate Europe team had hoped to be able to work with a thematic coordinator but soon realised the need for more general coordination. All other teams started with a responsible coordinator from the beginning. None have stopped or diminished the role of the coordinator.

The smaller teams mention oral agreements among team members concerning the general questions: 'it's based upon trust', says, for example, Goslinga from the ad-hoc Security for Sale investigation. Larger teams mention more explicit agreements, for example, a workflow-document the initiating members of the EIC network developed and all members agree on. Sometimes media partners demand contracts concerning liabilities and finances (Goslinga). For decision-making often the coordinators prepare material for a general discussion and the necessary decision in a larger part of or indeed the entire network.

There generally appears to be a strong wish to reach unanimous decisions or indeed, as a minimum, decisions which all team members can accept as reasonable. In the EIC network each partner has one vote – be that a small non-profit journalism centre or a large news magazine from a large country. 'It makes people more considerate to each other. If they behave like a despot now, others may do so too', says Candea.

However, the level of detail where all need to participate in a decision and the distinction between editorial and other matters are mentioned. An understanding of the structure of a given network is indispensable when attempting to carve out the decision-making.

The ICIJ is the largest of the networks examined here. It consists of a core team – until 2016 a unit within the Center for Public Integrity and since then as an independent non-profit organisation under US law. The ICIJ works with more than 80 media partners in more than 100 countries. The work rhythm throughout the research phase is set by weekly meetings. Coordination tasks within the core team are not carried out by a single person but are delegated: 'I have the helicopter responsibility', says Marina Walker. A data editor and regional coordinators of the ICIJ team have their respective fields of responsibility. The ICIJ decides on general questions such as publication date, team, and partners, as well as internal rules of working together. Besides that, media partners or journalists are free to work on their stories as they wish. 'When you start messing with the editorial independence, you get in trouble', she says. The ICIJ thus functions with a central core team assisting and coordinating the comparably large number of partners.

The EIC network does have a part-time coordinator but not a core team. Necessary competences are found within or on behalf of the entire network, a non-exclusive network around the 12 founding partners, and the work rhythm is a weekly telephone conference. With its 'one member one vote' approach, the EIC has experienced lengthy discussions occasionally. In case of deadlocks, the decision was made by the coordinator and the initiator of a given idea or the one who brought in a data-set, such as the journalist or intermediary who had negotiated with a given whistleblower. 'Usually the discussion is on specific findings – a finding by someone – any piece of information has an author', says Candea – and ultimately the initiator-principle could then be applied. While EIC thus works systematically with the idea of an initiator, network members can work in smaller groups within the network or bring in relevant partners to work with in sub-networks.

The Investigate Europe team consists of nine journalists making decisions together. Two weekly conversations – one on the ongoing investigation and one on general matters – provide the work rhythm for decision-making. In reality some of the minor decisions – such as assignments to a photographer for a few hundred euros – are made by the coordinator who informs the team and – if no one objects – assigns the task. In its first year all team members worked closely together on all topics. One team member adopts each topic and has a coordinating role preparing for meetings on that specific investigation, yet decisions are still made by all team members.

The two ad-hoc teams had less frequent contact. Both teams mention frequent bilateral correspondence between coordinator(s) and team combined with a monthly meeting in the Migrants Files team and a weekly newsletter summing up findings in the Security for Sale team.

Decision-Making and Structure Patterns

While some decisions are taken by either the initiator or coordinator or both, there is a general attempt to reach shared decisions welcomed or at least acceptable by all. Here the role of the coordinator is that of preparing and suggesting solutions.

The initiator of an investigation – be that by topic or data trove – holds a particular role not only when it comes to team composition but also on decision-making.

Recurring points on what needs attention to make decisions *about* were: team composition, the general set-up and work flow, the topic or material to work with (initiator), the publication date, and the multiple editorial decisions concerning a given investigation. In some set-ups funding and spending was a team decision.

The question of ownership of the research material – be that a leaked data-set or material gathered based upon a working hypothesis – was addressed only in connection with the role of the 'initiator'. Ownership of editorial material potentially needs not only editorial consideration but also legal, commercial, or ethical decisions.

Assuming that cross-border and other collaborative journalism arrangements are likely to grow in number and popularity, it makes sense to suggest a closer study of networking structures. Three set-ups emerge from these case studies: a core team assisting partners, a network with sub-groups, and a team of equal partners cooperating on all decisions and tasks. Already within the small sample of cases mentioned here at least one team – Investigate Europe – is about to move from the team of equal partners to the network with sub-groups model without changing in size. It's helpful for practitioners to understand the functioning, advantages, and disadvantages of these different models.

Related to the structure is – obviously – the technology for the communication and sharing of documents and data within the team. Technology is considered a task for the coordinator, and recurring features are an overall need for secure communication, document sharing, team communication – by mail or chat – as well as a sharing of findings as the research progresses. One coordinator prepared weekly newsletters to make sure all team members were aware of the status (Goslinga), one coordinator is in the process of preparing an internal handbook to make sure terminology, for example in updating a wiki on findings, is used consistently (Candea), while one group has a team function for it (ICIJ). The centralisation or decentralisation of a network thus must be reflected in the tech structure of the internal communication models while still safeguarding the necessary security levels.

The Role and Tasks of the Editorial Coordinator

Once the structure and general work procedure of a given team are set up, the role of the coordinator focuses on the day-to-day. In this section the tasks will be described including – where relevant – ethical and legal considerations. So how do the coordinators perceive their role?

'It's back and forth between the role of coordinating and guiding – that means when there is a dispute, different opinions – I show what is available, what are pros and cons, then people decide', says Stefan Candea of the EIC project about his role. 'It's both being an editor – and more than being an editor, being a reporter but more than being a reporter', says Marina Walker of ICIJ. 'It's a leadership role', says Elisa Simantke of Investigate Europe.

The tasks described by the coordinators resemble each other: calling and preparing face-to-face meetings (all); preparing and moderating the regular video conferences (Walker, Candea, Simantke); sharing information on the team via an internal newsletter (Goslinga, Gruhnwald/Kayser-Bril); contact with media outlets (Walker, Candea, Goslinga, Simantke); keeping the contact to tech and admin including fundraising; dealing with legal and fact-checking questions (Walker, Candea, Gruhnwald/Kayser-Bril); preparing and proposing discussion papers ahead of meetings for the teams to decide and coordinating follow-up (all); preparing a 'post-mortem' evaluation after each project (Candea); external communication about the project such as a blog, website, social media; translations, info-graphics, etc. in relation to publication; bringing team members to, for example, the European Investigative Journalism Conference (Candea, Goslinga).

Tasks appear to be similar throughout teams with only slight differences between teams with a long-term perspective and ad-hoc teams related to the technical set-up for internal communication; slight differences depending on team size and structure when it comes to opportunity to delegate and need to oversee.

Ethical and legal questions are an obvious item on the editorial coordinators' to-do lists. Providing general guidelines (Walker, Candea) and moderating case-by-case questions concerning – for example – the use of hidden camera (Walker), fact-checking, and confrontation – not least the timing of confrontation (Walker, Simantke, Gruhnwald/Kayser-Bril, Candea) and indeed the sources of and transparency about external funding (Simantke, Goslinga).

All coordinators interviewed had either faced or considered legal questions and described their role as coordinating between team members and being the ones who made sure necessary expertise was consulted. Dealing with differences in media legislation or national ethical guidelines on for example the mentioning of names of individuals or companies were cited as part of coordinator routines (Gruhnwald/Kayser-Bril). The ICIJ was slightly different as they apply legal scrutiny to the material the ICIJ core team provides to partners, while partners are responsible for their own legal situation and work.

With the slight differences connected to the structures of the teams, the tasks of the editorial coordinators appear to resemble each other, or – as Candea sums it up, 'it's a business management approach – entangled with journalism planning'. Going one level further in the descriptions, the quality of the communication, including considerations about editorial tradition and cultural background, demand special mention.

Communication and Cultural Differences

'Love all but row your own boat', said senior Swedish investigative and cross-border pioneer, Fredrik Laurin (Alfter 2015). This approach of respecting the different ways of practising journalism while staying responsible towards one's own audience, legal and ethical guidelines was confirmed throughout the interviews for this chapter. All teams thus obviously did make their journalism work. Yet communication and dealing with differences – intercultural and others – were mentioned among obstacles to getting from idea to publication. In order to get a better understanding of the various aspects, it makes sense to understand and contextualise communication and particularly communication in international teams.

Luckily journalists do not have to start from scratch, as other disciplines such as business sociology, psychology, and law also deal with general and intercultural communication practice (Alfter 2016). Business sociologists have tried to understand communication and cooperation across cultures for decades, with two schools on how to approach the challenge: the functionalist school – mapping and categorising national differences – and the interpretative school which favours 'experience and dialogue rather than pre-conceived opinions about "the Other"' (Askehave et al. 2009). Interviewees indeed mentioned the need for intercultural communication: 'You have to know how different cultures work, you may not be surprised when northern people don't celebrate at all, or when the other countries tend to overpromise, or when some are less strict in working with an organisation' (Kayser-Bril). Joking and irony were mentioned in that context as potential for serious misunderstandings. More frequently, differences were mentioned relating to varying journalism cultures (obviously in practice but more substantially also in role perception, a notion addressed by scholars like the Danish researchers Meyer and Brink Lund (2008)).

Interpersonal communication on a team working over long geographical distances and different editorial interpretations were emphasised most frequently by the interviewees.

Interpersonal Communication

Already in the team selection the ICIJ asks about a potential partner's wish and ability to work on a team, and Walker emphasises the 'added difficulty of remoteness' in cross-border teams. Besides looking for team players, the ICIJ has a 'zero tolerance' approach to 'passive aggressive' or 'snarky comments', and the coordinator would follow up immediately to safeguard a 'tone of inclusiveness and respect' and to address any problems 'in a straightforward manner' – either in the team or bilaterally between coordinator and team member/partner. 'If you do not moderate, and if you do not have those standards and if you do not have people who can embrace those kinds of standards, it can spiral into aggression, nervousness, insecurity', says Walker, who also emphasises the need for a coordinator who is a 'balanced and open person'.

An open communication is also highlighted by Candea of the EIC team, stressing that disagreements have to be discussed openly in the team. 'We lay out arguments, people may be furious or pissed, but they say so openly, they put it into the round. After this is done, there is room for cordiality, you don't take the debate in the back doors, back channels, you do not try to influence and take political fights' (Candea). After each publication the EIC team takes a 'post-mortem' analysis of what went well and what did not. In order to avoid 'stereotyping' of the colleagues, it is 'valuable to challenge each other's bias', however 'consuming' it may be. 'It's a cultural and a personal thing', says Candea, with cultural indicating more than national background. When a female, freelance journalist from a low-income country challenges a senior investigative editor at a large Western European medium, factors like gender, geography, and status play a role.

> People forget their newsroom roles when they are in (a team) conversation. But if you as a person are in a comfort position, you act differently. It's about your status of mind. If you are in a big organisation, you are in a position of leading people, you'll discuss in a different way compared to a freelancer from a poor country working from a basement. It's about the way you look at yourself.

To overcome such diversities in a constructive way a diverse group is needed and the group needs to be small enough to have a meaningful exchange. 'People need to feel safe', says Candea.

Also the smaller team mentioned the need to pay attention to communication before reaching editorial decisions, for example: it's a 'long process with several discussions' (Simantke).

Editorial Practice

While enjoying an experience of 'fruitful' cooperation once colleagues shared their findings, Simantke of Investigate Europe experienced difficulties in making colleagues share their findings in the team's sharing platforms. She relates this to the obstacle of having to translate and summarise in other languages but also to the habit of individual journalists to carry on researching until shortly before publication, while in cross-border teams the coordinator has to make sure information and material are spread within the team at the earliest possible stage.

Gruhnwald and Kayser-Bril of the Migrants Files team report issues with varying journalism practices, for example on fact-checking and delivering on time. Gruhnwald says:

> We had issues there, which is normal in a team with cultural differences, different understanding of media law, ethics. ... We had to establish

common ground. ... We had a different understanding on what an investigation should entail, what quality of information, what proof needed to publish.

As a solution, Kayser-Bril mentions their approach was to focus the journalistic work on an angle or a particular aspect and then all work in that direction.

Team communication and editorial decisions and standards are paramount in all teams. Communication, editorial practice, and understanding of the role of journalists are all mentioned by interviewees as being related to cultural differences with a broad definition of culture.

Perceived Needed Competences for Editorial Coordinators in Cross-Border Collaborative Journalism Teams

'Being a journalist and being a manager' (Simantke) would be the seven-word summary of competences of the editorial coordinator as perceived by all interviewed coordinators.

Both experience of actually doing cross-border, investigative journalism and the experience of coordinating or indeed being a leader in an editorial context were mentioned explicitly as key competences by almost all interviewees – with the added remark that one 'should be free of the need or the wish to dig into everything yourself'. Cross-border investigative journalism experience is crucial, according to Candea and others. 'It's a new field, we are just getting to know what the problems are, it's based on experience and needs further testing. Without the Scoop experience and the Offshore Leaks experience I would be worthless', says Candea, referring to the Danish-initiated Scoop project in Southeast and Eastern Europe and his work as part of the ICIJ team. 'I have tried hands-on and non-hands-on, I have tried different contexts, and I have tried hierarchical and non-hierarchical teams', he says.

Project management skills are emphasised by all interviewees: structuring, communicating, coordinating, 'seeing problems before anyone else', functioning as intermediary between journalism team and publishers, admin, and/or donors are mentioned widely. 'Project management is really the core, and it is not taught in any journalism school', says Kayser-Bril.

Understanding of different cultures is explicitly mentioned among competences by two of the coordinators, understanding of the technological and structural set-up of a workspace for a team by three.

Further individual remarks on perceived needed competences and considerations for coordinators were 'availability – if people have questions, you need to be ready to answer immediately, this should not be underestimated. If even small questions get a quick reply, you feel you are part of a team' (Goslinga). The support of the editor-in-chief was emphasised by a coordinator working in a newsroom (Goslinga) and trust in team members (Goslinga). Marina Walker of the ICIJ emphasised that the coordinator needs to have a 'balanced personality', be a 'team player and an excellent communicator'. She also emphasised an 'inclination of service: you are helping others, you are not the star, you are not the centre, you are facilitating.'

This leads to considerations about the role of the coordinator, which was commented on by two interviewees. Marina Walker mentioned the need for 'that editor's vision, the capacity of leading others'. It has to be 'a strong leader, so people would follow you, trust you and respect the decisions you, make', while also emphasising the need to be 'a leader who serves, and who is hands-on in the interest of the team'. The other coordinator who mentioned a view on his role was Stefan Candea from EIC, who aims to be a 'guide rather than a coordinator'. He perceives it as 'impossible to have a leader, make a plan and follow it. You need experience like a guide in the mountains on how to deal with ever new situations to address, something that you learnt from other guides.' 'The guide knows how to push people, how to connect them.' Also he emphasises the need of having outside-of-newsroom experience, 'otherwise you have a hierarchy-experience and will not serve the networks but one of the partners'.

Summing up on perceived competences, interviewees agree on the need for experience with journalism practice and editorial coordination practice as well as a strong need for project management skills. Insights into technical collaboration tools as well as insights into cultural differences and communication are desired competences. When it comes to describing the role of the coordinator as leader or guide, the two interviewees use different terminology which may indicate different role perceptions or indeed differently structured teams.

Summary and Conclusion

Cross-border collaborations of journalists have proven a powerful approach to investigative journalism and the method is applied by a variety of teams.

For this chapter teams of varying characters have been studied through interviews with the respective coordinators of these teams. All teams had one (in one case two) editorial coordinators, and initially had aimed for a flat structure with only a thematic coordinator. The term 'editorial coordinator' was applied by all. In several teams the journalist or organisation who had brought in a data-set or initiated a topic played a special role and gained more influence (in this chapter the term 'initiator' has been applied).

The interviewees described tasks, routines, and structures to provide a basis to understanding the necessary competences and indeed role of editorial coordinators. Answering the overall question 'New method, new skill, new position?' indeed there appears to be a new position – that of editorial coordinator with particular skills in coordinating teams with remote work places, from different journalistic traditions and so forth.

The role perceptions in this small sample of interviews – and thus in no way conclusive – appeared to correlate with different structures of the cross-border teams.

There was general agreement among the interviewees that practical experience in journalism (including investigative and cross-border) and practical experience with coordinating journalism teams was an asset or even crucial. Project management skills, including an understanding of the necessary technical tools, were emphasised widely as a necessity.

Throughout the interviews different journalism traditions and cultural differences in terms of communication and teamwork were acknowledged as an integrated part of the work and indeed in some cases an obstacle to be addressed in the day-to-day proceedings.

Three questions for further research come to mind to support future initiatives in collaborative decision-making. In informal structures (as several of these networks are), what are the legal and editorial implications of ownership of and responsibility for editorial material? Similarly, the structure of the *teams* and the *technical* structure has to be fully understood for well-informed decisions in editorial coordination.

Assuming that the method of cross-border journalism will be used more widely, the aim should be to work towards supporting journalists to become editorial coordinators in cross-border journalism teams. This includes – besides journalism and journalism management practice – project management skills, insights into journalism models and insights into intercultural communication.

4

Collaboration – One Tool among Many

Nicolas Kayser-Bril

The Panama Papers were a worldwide sensation in 2016. If we had Academy Awards for journalism, they'd be *Titanic* and *La La Land* rolled into one. Beyond the many records the projects broke, observers were struck by the collaborative nature of the effort. Hundreds of journalists worked together for months to produce ground-breaking reporting on tax evasion. The Panama Papers are not alone. The Russian Laundromat is a recent story coordinated by OCCRP, a non-profit. It brought together 60 journalists.[73] I had the chance to coordinate a group of over 20 journalists in 2014 and 2015 in the Migrants' Files, an investigation on the number of men and women who died in their attempt to reach Europe.

Such collaborations were successful. To produce successful stories, the thinking goes, journalists should collaborate more. This syllogism is attractive, but I doubt it's true. I have coordinated many unsuccessful collaborations as well. The Belarus Networks failed because of a lack of involvement from a key partner. Turkish Puppets failed because the publication partners could not grasp why the story was important.[74] Two or three other collaborations I was part of also failed to reach their initial goal.

Informed by a few successes and many failures, this text argues that we should consider collaborations in journalism for what they are: a tool among others that should be used only when appropriate.

Media companies joining forces is not something new. Back in the first part of the 19th century, newspapers in the United States pooled

---

[73] http://www.beobachter.ch/wirtschaft/artikel/geldwaesche_die-schweiz-als-drehscheibe/

[74] Our story showed how European governments refuse to consider Muslims of Turkish descent as full-fledged citizens, allowing the Turkish government to meddle in their religious and cultural affairs. European-Turks who refuse to be treated as pawns in a geopolitical game are ostracised by both European and Turkish authorities. Most of our media partners were fully unable to process a story that involved Muslims who were neither 'terrorists' nor 'moderates'. I blame the lack of diversity in their newsrooms, though plain racism is probably also at play.

resources to maintain a pony express service (a kind of Uber, for horse-carried messages). From the 1850s onwards, they institutionalised their collaboration by sharing a telegraph service. They created a joint venture to buy a steamer boat, itself a new and very expensive technology, that would fetch the mail directly from ocean-going ships arriving from Europe at their first American stop at Halifax, Canada. The fresh news was then telegraphed (an even newer technology) from Boston to New York, where each newspaper would run it. That's how the Associated Press was born (Schwarzlose 1989: 80ff.).

A theory goes that this early collaboration was just a cartel meant to put other telegraph lines between Boston and New York out of business. But it's not my point. My point is that this joint effort was driven by a necessity to share a piece of equipment, much like some media companies use the printing facilities of their competitors.[75]

I haven't found examples of explicitly collaborative journalistic projects in the 19th and 20th century.[76] The Muckrakers of the Roosevelt era in the United States, who pioneered investigative journalism as we know it, worked alone or in pairs (Weinberg and Shaffer-Weinberg 2001). In 1973, Bob Woodward and Carl Bernstein of Watergate fame did not rush to share Deep Throat's material with other newsrooms. Europe's first data-driven investigator, E. D. Morel, did work in collaboration with others as he documented slavery in the Congo in the first years of the 20th century. He used pictures taken by missionaries to complement his data-driven analyses. However, this was never a joint effort – more of an alliance between activists.

Collaboration in journalism is a new thing, which began in the late 2000s. Wikileaks pioneered the method when it brought together the *New York Times*, the *Guardian,* and *Der Spiegel* in 2010 over the Afghan War Diaries, a database documenting war crimes by NATO troops in Afghanistan.[77] The method spread widely and is now considered normal whenever a major international story is released.

There are good reasons to go into a collaboration. In the case of the Afghan War Diaries or the Panama Papers, a coordinating organisation offered exclusive material to newsrooms. The coordinating entity offered technical skills that newsrooms did not possess and pooled the reporting.

---

[75] https://www.nzz.ch/wirtschaft/nzz-druckzentrum-wird-geschlossen-1.18474785

[76] There's an exception. In 1976, 18 reporters got together in Phoenix, Arizona, to investigate the murder of a journalist.

[77] Wikileaks was the turning point, but Journalismfund.eu was already insisting on cross-border collaborations a couple of years before 2010.

Finally, it ensured that all partners published jointly, so that the joint publication itself became a news story.

This process is bold and brilliant. It is not, however, especially innovative. Rather, it is the adaptation to journalism of an ideology that favours networks over structures, which permeated the business world a couple of decades ago.

The ideal career of the 20th century was to remain loyal to a company for 40 years, regularly climbing the hierarchical ladder. Since the 1980s, this ideal has changed dramatically. To be considered successful now means having a large network of contacts that one can activate for a specific project, hopping from one network configuration to the next according to one's current needs.[78]

The appearance of the network as the best way to run an enterprise (be it a business or an investigation) fits perfectly with the idea that a system works best when individuals can apply their skills where they are most needed. Instead of building an organisation that possesses all the possible skills it will ever need, it's more efficient to look for a specific person possessing a specific skill for a specific need. The emphasis on individuals, as opposed to organisations, is one of the basic tenets of neoliberalism, the ideology that became hegemonic in the 1980s and has remained ever since.

The conservative nature of journalism ensured that this 'new spirit' entered only slowly in the newsroom,[79] but it's slowly creeping in. Private donors lead the pack in demanding that the journalistic projects they fund be collaborative. JournalismFund.eu, for instance, offers grants only to cross-border teams. The same applies to Connecting Continents, another grant programme run by the same organisation. JournalismGrants, a programme funded by the Bill and Melinda Gates Foundation, is less insistent on collaboration but mentions that 'teams' should apply. The Volkswagen Stiftung recently asked that journalists team up with scientists.

Donor-funded outlets that operate outside of newsrooms also insist that they are *networks* or *consortia*, not publishers. The Organised Crime and Corruption Reporting Project and the International Consortium of Investigative Journalists are the most visible and successful, but many other sexist at a smaller scale or at regional levels (Arab Reporters for Investigative Journalism for Arabic-speaking countries, the Balkan Investigative Reporting Network for the Balkans, etc.). Public donors also consider

---

[78] This is a very condensed summary of Boltanski and Chiapello 2006.

[79] On the inherently conservative nature of newsrooms, Jane Jacobs (1992: 208) makes a great point.

collaboration a prerequisite for funding. The European Commission recently awarded grants for journalism where they requested that applying consortia be made up of at least four members but wrote that the more members in the consortium, the better.[80]

This is not to say that collaboration is bad – or good. But it did not arise in an ideological vacuum. It might be the case that collaboration emerged out of the needs of journalists who found a new way to organise. It might also be the case that the profession is just following a trend from the business world without giving it much thought.

Collaboration is the action of achieving a precise goal with a group of persons without creating a new organisation. Everything lies in the 'precise goal'. If the purpose of the collaboration is uncertain or changing, the glue binding the team together won't hold.

To state the obvious, the more interesting the documents that support the collaborative investigation, the more likely it is that the collaboration will be successful. If, on the contrary, the collaboration is not based on existing material but builds a story from the ground up, it will fail as soon as the initial goal moves out of view.

This can happen if the topic of the investigation isn't clear. When we worked on the costs of Fortress Europe with the Migrants' Files consortium, for instance, we set out to investigate who benefited from policies that prevented men and women from claiming asylum in Europe (walls, fences, electronic gadgets that sniff out people attempting to cross a border, etc.). It turned out that 'making money from Fortress Europe' was extremely complex to delineate, and harder still to investigate. If everyone's mission is not perfectly defined, collaborative work becomes arduous.

More commonly, collaborations falter when the initial plan is changed. It happened that we based a collaboration on data that we were supposed to obtain through a freedom of information request. When it did not succeed, the whole project had to be revamped. Projects can also derail upon publication if a media partner misinterprets the documents that are made available by the coordinating partner, for instance. In rarer cases, partners can also fail to carry out their part of the agreed-upon work.

Collaborative projects have costs. Running a consortium requires good project management skills and enormous amounts of energy. The larger the project and the less clear the goal, the more so. Sometimes, these extra costs

---

[80] The Commission required 'the involvement of as many media/journalists as possible'. http://ec.europa.eu/newsroom/dae/document.cfm?doc_id=17413

outweigh the benefits of a collaboration and the project would be better done by a single person or a single organisation.

Collaboration by itself does not make a journalistic project better. Sometimes, it can seriously hamper it by making it less able to cope with changes in the initial plan. It's high time for funders to stop requiring that applicants work collaboratively, especially if they require that a project be innovative at the same time. Innovation, by definition, means making use of new and, ergo, untested processes. This implies that the risks of failure are high, thereby increasing the costs of collaboration tremendously. As long as they combine both criteria, they secure the failure of their grantees.

Instead, they should ensure that a successful project can be replicated or translated quickly. To do so, they should spend less money on grants that are bound to fail (the ones that require both collaboration and innovation) and more money on helping journalists find possible post-publication partners.

In a nutshell, this means spending more money on conferences and other get-togethers and – more importantly – on ensuring that a diverse set of people attend them. Diversity means inviting minorities, of course, as well as working journalists who cannot find the time to leave their newsroom – a recurring problem at European conferences.[81]

---

[81] This short essay is a write-up of a contribution to the panel on 'Investigating big data: collaboration and best practice' at the Journalism Festival of Perugia of April 2017.

5

Investigative Journalism and Advocacy: Natural Allies?

Anne Koch

Corruption is global, ignores national borders, and mostly is secretive. It's based on a nimble network that helps wrongdoers hide ill-gotten gains in the shadows and it deepens global inequality. Governments spend millions, if not billions, on anti-corruption agencies, anti-fraud investigators, stockmarket monitoring, and financial intelligence units that chase money laundering.

Corruption is also the target of both investigative journalists and anti-corruption NGOs like Transparency International, Global Witness and others. My work at Transparency International (TI) has given me the chance to reflect on how journalists and advocates can work together and we're about to launch a collaborative initiative with the investigative journalism network, the Organised Crime and Corruption Reporting Project (OCCRP). TI has about a hundred national affiliates or 'chapters' around the globe working to combat corruption. OCCRP, for its part, is an investigative reporting platform formed by more than 40 non-profit investigative centres, scores of journalists, and several major regional news organisations across the world, who do transnational investigative reporting and promote technology-based approaches to exposing organised crime and corruption worldwide.

Investigative journalists are naming the corrupt, but too often there is little follow-up and the corrupt often get away with it. The new OCCRP–TI project is structured so that OCCRP will investigate and expose, and TI will take up a number of stories or cases and undertake advocacy and campaigning work around each case to press for longer-term change. Nevertheless, the partnership raises thorny issues about cooperation between investigative journalists and NGOs.

This chapter will address some of these issues in the context of the much analysed changing media landscape, a growing discussion about what journalism is and should be, and the growth of partnerships, specifically between journalists and NGOs. All of these subjects are vast in their own right and can only be touched upon briefly here. However, hopefully it will provide food for thought in a necessary and important debate, as well as suggest some criteria for successful collaboration.

Some years ago, as a senior manager at the BBC, I co-led a global investigation into the cross-border trade in asbestos with the International Consortium of Investigative Journalists, *Dangers in the Dust: Inside the Global Asbestos Trade* (ICIJ 2010). White asbestos, which the industry prefers to label as chrysotile, historically the most common form and the only kind of asbestos still in use, is a cancer-causing fibre which kills about 100,000 workers a year according to the International Labour Organization, as a result of asbestos-related diseases. The World Health Organization says that 125 million workers are still exposed to asbestos and some experts think that by 2030 asbestos will have taken as many as 10 million lives around the world (WHO 2014: 2). While asbestos is banned or restricted in much of the world, it is aggressively marketed in developing countries. Our joint investigation revealed the tactics used by the makers of asbestos building materials to market their products to poorer countries despite overwhelming evidence of the mineral's lethality. The multiple cases and stories produced by the partnership made substantial impact: the findings were not only covered by about 250 media outlets in more than 20 languages but were used by public health activists and concerned politicians in countries such as Brazil, India, Mexico, and Canada.

ICIJ has compiled evidence of the impact the collaboration made; they do this routinely.[82] At the time, and later reviewing the impact, I thought that we could have been more systematic in the way we collaborated and shared information during and after the journalism was published. And as a journalist, this was by no means the first time I had pause for thought about how we might increase our impact.

With this variety of experience, from mainstream broadcaster to campaigning organisation, the often-discussed blurring of roles between activists, citizen journalists, watchdogs, and journalists is something that I often reflect on. I also experience it on a daily basis. This chapter is based on that experience, and on personal and public discussions about the

---

[82] See https://www.icij.org/tags/impact

relationship between investigative journalists, publishers and broadcasters, and NGO representatives.

The truism is that investigative journalists throw a spotlight onto corrupt individuals and networks, forcing the truth into the open; activists then generate heat by pressuring governments and law enforcement to act and by mobilising citizens to press for change, even to go to the streets. In this view, they are separate professions motivated by different factors.

Yet in reality, the relationship between investigative journalists and NGOs, whether working on corruption or other issues, has always been more complex and nuanced because their roles often overlap. For as long as I can remember this has been debated and worried over, with claims that the relationship needed redefinition.[83] Both require – or should require – rigorous evidence and both seek the truth. Both are prepared, at least sometimes, to exchange information when it is timely and with those they trust. Importantly, both also aim not only to give citizens the information they need but also to hold the powerful accountable. They work together in media all over the world, though many, especially in North America and Western Europe, are reluctant to discuss this too openly. There is a long history of both collaboration and antagonism between the two, but due to wider changes briefly touched upon below, there has been a massive blurring of the lines. The relationship between the two, it is argued here, should be discussed more widely, made more transparent, and with careful calibration there is greater room for cooperation – without a concomitant loss of independence or integrity.

In June 2017, US marshals took into custody former Panamanian President Ricardo Martinelli, who had fled his country and been living in a luxury home in Miami. His former government is at the centre of more than 200 investigations into corruption in multiple countries, with about a dozen cases in which he personally is alleged to have played a central role – for which he now faces extradition (Prensa 2017). One of these cases took place in 2011–12 when dozens of children in Panama were poisoned after being served glass-like plastic shards and excessive amounts of sodium in their school meals – the results of an inflated contract, the proceeds of which were allegedly skimmed off by Martinelli and his associates (Newsroom Panama 2015). So far he has escaped justice for these and other alleged acts of corruption; at least US$100 million in public funds may have been lost during the ex-president's administration due to corruption (Prisma 2015).

---

[83] These are too numerous to list, but for a drop in the bucket see Lashmar 2011, 2014; Nieman Foundation 2009–10; Waisbord 2011.

Also in June 2017, the trial opened in Paris of Teodoro Nguema Obiang Mangue, the high-living vice-president of Equatorial Guinea and son of the country's president. Obiang is suspected of accumulating a vast fortune from embezzled funds which enabled him to buy property in Paris, Malibu, and Brazil, luxury cars, works of art, not to speak of his collection of Michael Jackson memorabilia (*Guardian* 2017). In the United States, Obiang relinquished US$30 million in real estate and luxury goods to settle a lawsuit brought by the US Department of Justice (DoJ 2014). Undeterred, the younger Obiang was last seen in Rio de Janeiro where, living it up during Carnival, he booked more than 30 suites at Copacabana Palace, each one costing more than US$2,000 a night (*Folha de S.Paulo* 2015). No one seriously believes he acquired these goods on his government salary in a country where about three-quarters of the population lives in poverty and which is regularly criticised by human rights groups for its repressive laws, unlawful killings, and use of torture. He is on trial in France for embezzling more than US$112 million of state money to fund a lavish lifestyle in the French capital (OCCRP 2017).

In both cases journalists (and investigative journalists specifically) and NGOs have played an essential role in bringing these cases to light and the Obiang case to court.

In the Martinelli case TI has worked hard to convince journalists, at least those outside Panama, as well as Panamanian and US investigators, that an old corruption story continues to be important and newsworthy – meanwhile the alleged perpetrator so far has escaped justice, living in luxury abroad.

In the Obiang case, two non-governmental organisations – Transparency International France and SHERPA, a French legal NGO – started the investigation in 2007. When they, along with an association of Congolese citizens abroad, filed a criminal complaint against Obiang and against two other African heads of state, from Gabon and Congo-Brazzaville, they accused the three African leaders of buying assets and properties in France with proceeds from corruption and embezzlement. The Obiang case, which has become known in France as that of 'Bien mal acquis' or 'ill-gotten gains', specifically represents ten years of painstaking work. It kicked off a legal battle that many considered lost from the start. The objective is to return the stolen money to its rightful owners, the people of Equatorial Guinea.[84]

Although the court case in Paris focuses on the purchasing of French

---

[84] In the process, TI France also produced advice to NGOs who wish to work on similar cases: see briefing documents (2008, 2011).

property with embezzled funds, Obiang's alleged corrupt activities played out across the world, with legal seizures from a mansion in Malibu, a garage full of cars in Geneva, and yachts taken to dry docks in the Netherlands and Morocco (Quartz 2016). Thus, while NGO lawyers singled out the who and the how, the pursuit of this story has involved many journalists on multiple continents.[85] And the pattern is reciprocal – journalists expose what the lawyers and advocates can later pursue.

The relationship between journalists and NGOs described above is not new, and dozens of examples could be found daily in almost every country. However, the effects of digital disruption, with the explosion of choice, the empowerment as many would see it of audiences, and their influence on the agenda, and the low levels of trust for journalists, have muddied the waters. In the context, too, of the dominance of the tech giants, the decline in revenue and disappearance of once reliable business models in a mere decade, not to mention the general decline in traditional journalism,[86] the line between professionally trained journalists and alternative investigation and newsgathering has blurred. The economics fuels this trend as has been well documented; some of the money has gone online, sometimes to fake news.

Much investigative journalism is now being carried out by relatively small organisations: NGOs that raise funds from foundations, private donors, companies, and governments, a trend that started in the mid-1970s but has accelerated with the collapse of orthodox business models. In addition, one recent wide-ranging study of note has documented the growth of what its authors call, 'stakeholder driven media' (SDM), a 'stunning range of actors who control their own media and use those media to directly affect individuals, communities, organisations and society' (Hunter et al. 2016: 5). This is at the expense of the mainstream media (MSM), who have lost their share of previous agenda-setting influence at the expense of the SDM (Hunter et al. 2016: 10). This has been accompanied unsurprisingly by a sometimes hostile debate about what journalism is and who is qualified to do it, and the increasing and unprecedented threats to journalists the world over[87] where the challenges are huge and varied and include intimidation, violence, media concentration, and political control.

---

[85] For a more detailed account of the French case see the OSF report. The part on civil society support for the proceedings is particularly interesting and shows the added-value specialised NGOs can bring (2015: 13).

[86] With all the changes, it has become so difficult to estimate how many journalism jobs have been lost that the American Society of News Editors has given up trying (Poynter 2016).

[87] See European Union Agency for Fundamental Rights report (FRA 2016) or the Committee to Protect Journalists report (CPJ 2017).

Journalists in parts of the media, particularly in North America and Europe, have long relied on a shield of impartiality or objectivity and adhere to strict editorial guidelines when dealing with campaigners, charities, and other NGOs.[88] Impartiality as defined by the BBC, as its head of news has argued, 'is not the same as objectivity or balance or neutrality ... [a]t its simplest it means not taking sides ... about providing a breadth of view' (BBC Academy 2017). This is at odds with the mission of NGOs. But the concepts of impartiality and objectivity are increasingly questioned,[89] and proponents for a so-called post-impartial world are growing, as are the number of journalists who speak openly and often critically about the constraints of impartiality.[90]

At the same time there is a growing debate about whether truth and transparency rather than neutrality should be in the forefront.[91] It is broadly accepted that some of the biggest media outlets are highly partisan and have never aspired to impartiality, happy to defend their agendas in the name of independence – and many consumers seek that out. Furthermore, government and commercial interference has long been widespread in the media, challenging independence, and true impartiality. Underlying what is a worthy quest for impartiality is a belief that those with an agenda are not interested in the truth (see Steele 2010). The fact is that other organisations are investigating and publishing research and casework they hold to be as strong as the best investigative journalism. And they have an audience who may or may not distinguish between their findings and that of traditional journalists – another reason why this issue needs to be grappled with.

In many if not most parts of the world, the liberal Western model of the necessary separation between journalism and activism is not understood, let alone recognised – one literally can be a journalist in the morning, an activist in the afternoon, and a blogger in the evening. I discussed this with young journalists and activists in Moscow, to cite one example, and they didn't understand my concern with the blurring of lines. Although I don't have any hard evidence, I would guess that the majority of news media

---

[88] See e.g. BBC's Editorial Guidelines section 4; numerous articles but to cite a very recent one: Boaden (2017).

[89] See Jay Rosen's *View from Nowhere*: he describes this as 'a bid for trust that advertises the viewlessness of the news producer. Frequently it places the journalist between polarised extremes, and calls that neither-nor position impartial' (2010).

[90] See recent reflections e.g. by Paul Mason, to cite only one contribution of many.

[91] See articles by Phil Harding, Mark Thompson and many others. The former BBC News boss Richard Sambrook has asked 'Does a neutral voice hold the same value today as it did a century ago? Is the emphasis on impartiality in news actually an impediment to a free market in ideas?' (2012), and David Weinberger has stated that 'Transparency brings us to reliability the way objectivity used to' (2009).

around the world are prepared to give by-lines to NGO researchers and investigators.

The work of NGOs in the area of journalism and investigative journalism is important, too, where there is a lot of media concentration or where media freedom is weak or non-existent, as has been well documented.[92] Even in Brazil, where there is media freedom and relatively good media outlets, media concentration is a particular problem in some states and municipalities. According to a study conducted by the NGO Transparência Brasil, many of the owners of the Brazilian regional media (not only newspapers but also radio and TV) are front-line players in the political arena and allegedly involved in corruption (Abramo 2007). The output of such outlets is highly selective – corruption cases are rarely covered. In those environments a lot of the work on investigating and publicising corruption is thus done by NGOs.

It is in this context that TI and OCCRP struck up a novel partnership. The initiative is soon to be launched as the Global Anti-Corruption Consortium. As well as investigating stories, OCCRP will build a global networked platform, while TI will advocate and campaign for longer-term change. This might involve a national or global campaign; it might mean taking steps to try and ensure that the corrupt are prosecuted; in others it will be to try and address the systemic causes that lead to corruption – a corrupt judiciary, lax enforcement of money laundering laws, and others. TI hopes, too, where possible, to be able to seek redress for victims of cases of grand corruption. Both organisations also hope in time it will extend to other NGOs and investigative journalists because greater cooperation with other like-minded and independent NGOs is also needed. As Drew Sullivan, founder, editor, and director of OCCRP and TI partner, said to me, 'You have reporters investigate a problem. Then activists. Then police. In the three different investigations information is lost and knowledge is not passed through. It's inefficient. We need to share our information better.'

There is no doubt that the cooperation raises big issues – ethical issues, security issues, a clash of interests, and so on. However, in this project both TI and OCCRP are clear that cooperation will be enhanced further by mutual freedom and the maintenance of each party's independence, structured and flexible cooperation (not coordination per se), and trust. We will cooperate on the basis of clear evidence and data, with an understanding that each party has a different job to do. Cooperation will be limited and each organisation has its own staff, legal support, and objectives, and we have

---

[92] See Reporters Without Borders (2017).

clear protocols about sharing information. If there is a joint commitment to independence, truth, and transparency with each other and with audiences/constituencies about conflicts, as well as how successes are achieved, we hope the project will lead to greater impact. It should be noted that we are experimenting, and our collaboration may not be entirely new – we just want to make it more systematic.

This partnership is coalescing at a moment when many North American and Western European journalists increasingly have to contend with new colleagues who don't fit their assumptions of what a journalist is. Here again debates rage about what 'journalism' is and who is qualified to do it. Many people who neither have professional qualifications nor work in organisations with an editorial structure are out there writing and shaping public opinion – the two most read blogs during the UK election, for instance, were from non-journalists.[93]

On the other hand, however, trained journalists and researchers are being hired by campaigning, non-governmental organisations to publish investigative stories (Powers 2015). Entities trying out new models include, ProPublica, the Kaiser Foundation, and Open Secrets in the USA and some of the national chapters affiliated with TI in Russia, Honduras, Montenegro, and the Czech Republic – to cite a handful. Global Witness, for example, employs journalists and has both initiated and investigated major stories that have been picked up by major media outlets like the *Financial Times*, the *Guardian*, and ABC News.

Some would go even further in their diagnosis of what they describe as a crisis in journalism. Drew Sullivan from OCCRP believes that we are experiencing 'a Guttenberg moment' – and we must catch up with changing times. What we have traditionally called journalism is disappearing because of the above-mentioned blurring of roles between activists, bloggers, citizen journalists, watchdogs, and journalists. 'If you can't tell them apart, they are doing the same thing', states Sullivan. 'They are all investigators. Journalists don't need to be activists – we just need to agree on the findings.' He believes we need to define new roles and confront persistent corruption with 'truth,

---

[93] 'With seven days until Britain goes to the polls, a new force is shaping the general election debate. Highly partisan, semi-professional political blogs … [w]ebsites run by a publicity-shy English tutor in Yorkshire, an undergraduate student in Nottingham and a former management consultant in Bristol are publishing some of the most shared articles about the UK general election, ranking alongside and often above the BBC, the Guardian and the Independent … and have emerged as one of the most potent forces in election news sharing, according to research conducted for the Guardian by the web analytics company Kaleida. Two of the three most shared articles since Theresa May called the election on 18 April remain those written by Thomas Clark, who publishes left-leaning articles from his Yorkshire home under the moniker Another Angry Voice.' (Guardian 2017).

activism, and good policy, an enterprise that is at the heart of democracy, by building networks of like-minded investigators'. And this is why OCCRP is building a collaborative platform where journalists and NGOs can share information. 'Journalism ethics are important but so is the power and money of crime and corruption in the developing world. We're losing the battle. Badly.'[94]

Sullivan's colleague at OCCRP, Paul Radu, and I presented this initiative at a panel last December, the International Anti Corruption Conference. Radu began with the fact that corruption is deepening and increasingly globalised.

> *Investigative journalists have had some great successes like the Panama Papers ... and done some amazing work. But we're still doing too little. Look at the levels of corruption and organised crime – they are growing every day. The corrupt are so powerful they are effectively capturing governments and their collaboration across borders is far better than ours. What we're doing is like picking one cherry here, another there.*[95]

And while not everyone on the panel was convinced by the case made by Paul and I that more systematic cooperation is necessary, there was agreement that changes in the world of journalism necessitate new ways of thinking and working. The consensus was that not enough was being done either to investigate or combat corruption and that the relationship between NGO watchdogs and journalists needed rethinking and careful experimentation.

The journalists on the panel acknowledged that, as Dave Kaplan, Executive Director of the Global Investigative Journalism Network, put it, 'high quality investigations increasingly are being done by activists, often by former journalists now on their staff who find they have more time to focus on key issues'. Patrick Alley, co-founder of Global Witness, said that his organisation will continue to work on a case for years if necessary and this has brought them huge benefits in terms of impact. He argued against a false dichotomy between investigative journalism carried out by traditional media and that carried out by NGOs ('is journalism what you do, or who you work for') and disagreed with Kaplan's description of 'former' journalists; those on his staff, he said, regard themselves as working journalists.

---

[94] From personal conversations and a radio interview for PRI (Sullivan 2017).

[95] Conference panel: Journalists and Activists – More Light, More Heat. Panellists: Patrick Alley, director and co-founder, Global Witness; Carlos Hernandez, president of the Association for a More Just Society in Honduras and a TI chapter; Beatrice Edwards, international program director, Government Accountability Project (one of the main whistleblower protection organisations in the USA) and myself; Paul Radu, investigative journalist and director, OCCRP; David Kaplan, executive director, GIJN; and Marina Walker, deputy director, ICIJ (Dec. 2016).

The potential synergies are apparent. The pitfalls, however, are that journalists who are seen to campaign could risk the trust of their partners and readers – a serious danger in times when trust is closely linked to the objectives mentioned above: objectivity, impartiality, transparency, and neutrality. Nevertheless, it would be naïve not to acknowledge the blurring of lines and to work out how to address this.

Sometimes it's not even about blurred lines but shared core values. Marina Walker of ICIJ said that they often get input and knowledge from NGOs, but in a reporter–source relationship.

We are united by the idea that we want to change the world. That is part of the criteria when we make a decision about what work ICIJ should pursue. … But how do we draw a line? We will not take a position on any of the issues we have exposed; we will not invite the advocacy community to join in our research, such as full access to the Panama Papers, as there are too many risks, legal and other, and we have to control our material and our data. Advocates have told us that we help them more if we maintain clear lines of separation and roles. They have very different roles to ours.

Roles do diverge and complexity abounds: Beatrice Edwards spoke about the delicate relationship between protecting the interests of whistleblowers when working with the media.[96] Carlos Hernandez Martinez said that most media in Honduras was neither independent nor impartial and captured by corporate and other interests.[97] If there is no free media, good NGOs ought to then be taken seriously as researchers, investigators, and even journalists, echoing Alley's suggestion that we shouldn't get hung up on the distinctions. 'NGOs still have a role to play even if there is free media – look at TI, Global Witness's and others' exposés on all sorts of things – NGOs are a necessary addition to the mix, not a replacement for the media.'

Let's return to the main question: Why would an NGO like TI want to cooperate with investigative journalists?

The first reason is to share essential evidence and facts – it really is as basic

---

[96] Obviously not the main objective of journalists, though good journalists understand this issue well. There are very different interests and clear ground rules are critical but there is a great deal to be gained by collaborating.

[97] In Honduras, to avoid interference in investigation the TI chapter built up a large team of researchers. At first, because they couldn't get published in the mainstream media, they published their findings online. However, as internet access is limited, they started to produce technical papers to brief the media which would then publish the findings. The impact of some of the chapter investigations has been massive. http://asjhonduras.com/webhn/investigaciones

as that. Investigators (both journalists and law enforcement professionals) simply have more experience and know-how in investigating cases, and often journalists have been more open to sharing information than law enforcement agencies, although of course the latter play a role in the wider picture. Good investigative journalists provide documents and evidence, the material that NGOs need to do their advocating and campaigning. The Panama Papers case is an obvious recent example, as are the so-called Lux Leaks documents.[98] These cases gave rise to extensive work by some NGOs on whistleblowing policy and the role of accountancy firms as enablers of corruption and tax avoidance – numerous others could be cited.

A second vital reason is impact. Journalists often are better able to package and disseminate the findings, and to reach bigger audiences. When Global Witness carried out an undercover investigation of lawyers in New York City[99] and shared their findings with CBS's *60 Minutes* programme, this ensured an audience of millions. In other cases, it's about targeting a particular constituency of readers or viewers. Journalism also helps to shape public opinion against sleaze in government, scrutinises laws and regulations, and can in itself prompt governments to respond.

One of the most challenging areas in combating corruption is to figure out what has an impact – in short, what works. This is a complex question with few clear answers and many people have tried to grapple with it. There is evidence that investigative journalism makes a difference. There is the perhaps obvious and widely observed correlation between free media and less corruption that is mostly consistent.[100] One of the world's leading experts on corruption issues, Alina Mungiu-Pippidi, states that although historical context and development play a vital role (thus explaining the Nordic countries' relative lack of corruption) the two critical variants on stopping corruption are active and unrestrained civil society and free media (Mungiu-Pippidi 2015).

A key piece of evidence comes from Transparency International itself. It conducted an extensive survey of business management in 30 countries on the best ways to fight corruption. It gathered responses from 3,000 business people across 13 sectors that included real estate, banking, mining, and so on. The survey asked them to rank the effectiveness of six measures,

---

[98] See the ICIJ websites https://panamapapers.icij.org/ and https://www.icij.org/project/luxembourg-leaks/explore-documents-luxembourg-leaks-database. Also see https://www.transparency.org/news/pressrelease/transparency_international_calls_for_luxleaks_whistleblowers_to_be_exonerated

[99] Global Witness, 2017. https://www.globalwitness.org/shadyinc

[100] Studies backing this are almost too numerous to list. See e.g. Stapenhurst 2000; Mungiu-Pippidi 2015.

from corporate due diligence to national anti-bribery laws to international treaties. Investigative journalism came out on top: business people in 20 of the 30 countries surveyed chose investigative journalism as the most effective tool at fighting corruption. In 27 countries it was ranked higher than international agreements, and in 24 countries higher than national anti-bribery laws. This may well be because of the ability of investigative journalism to significantly raise reputational risk, and therefore increasing the reputational cost for corporate and political sectors of engaging in bad or corrupt practices which might get exposed (TI 2012).

The Global Investigative Journalism Network (GIJN), an international association of about 155 non-profit member organisations that support and produce investigative journalism in 68 countries, also has shown the impact it can make around the world.[101] Another very recent example is the work on American investigative journalism by James T. Hamilton, Hearst Professor of Communications at Stanford University, in his book, *Democracy's Detectives: The Economics of Investigative Journalism.*

OCCRP has its own impressive metrics in showing the impact on corruption of its journalism: more than US\$5.7 billion in assets frozen or seized by governments, more than 1,400 company closures, indictments, and court decisions; 84 criminal investigations and government inquiries launched as a result of its stories; and the list goes on. This was one of the many factors that led to the current collaboration with OCCRP, as was Drew Sullivan's view that exposure alone is not nearly as effective as working on the issues well past publication day. 'Name and shame doesn't work, because they have no shame anymore', he says. 'We call it hack and track. We basically use big data. We use investigative reporting, and we track them everywhere they go, and we show exactly what they're doing' (Sullivan 2017). Despite TI's research, the reality is that while an exposé can bring attention to an issue, raise the stakes, and even be a catalyst for change, it is following it up with persistent advocacy, public mobilisation, and other factors that most often leads to change. This is backed up by academic research.[102]

It is, of course, impossible to isolate the impact of either a free press or watchdog reporting from other factors that are linked to the control of corruption, such as whether a country can even boast rule of law, an independent judiciary, or respect for civil society among others (the targets of advocacy and campaigning). The impact of journalism can easily be blunted by many other forces. The role that investigative journalism plays is

---

[101] See http://impact.gijn.org.
[102] See Uslaner (2008), to cite only one example.

part of a wider picture which TI has compared to a complex machine with many interrelated parts: if one part isn't functioning, it can throw the whole machine out of kilter or stop it working altogether.

However, it is this relationship between what investigation can provide and the need to extend it to other organisations that led to the collaboration with TI. In fact, going back to my work at the BBC with the ICIJ on asbestos, the purpose of collaboration is the amplification of impact, whether between journalists or between journalists and campaigners. In a globalised world where reliable information is increasingly challenged, we could do more to raise our game and make greater impact. NGOs already provide a lot of research and expertise, analytical depth and case studies. They pick up cases when the journalists are finished, in effect creating a long tail to the story by advocating for change. This is at the heart of how they can improve impact.

Despite the blurring of lines that I have discussed, I remain convinced that there is a fundamental difference between journalists and NGO activists. Journalists shouldn't be campaigners and vice versa. They don't need to be. But to be effective, neither side can be complacent, or draw lines that limit real cooperation. In order to protect and enhance the important work of investigation done by civil society – whether it is by journalists, NGOs, or academics, who are under attack in many parts of the world, including in the US, and challenged by unprecedented levels and penetration of propaganda and false news – we need to experiment with new forms of collaboration.

Cooperation will be realised when there is more systematic sharing of evidence and data. Some of this data should also be made available to citizens who then can use it to get informed about issues affecting them directly. As Paul Radu put it,

> *The moment that journalists or activists expose data on corruption, creating a database of documents, then we stop the corrupt from doing business as usual. Banks won't give loans, and other companies won't do business with them. We get criminals writing us letters that say that we are costing them millions of dollars by adverse publicity, and asking us to take down our information. That database also allows us all to stick to the story and to revisit.* (IACC 2016)

Success in the future may well mean collaboration because shining a light on the corrupt requires combing and synthesising multiple information streams, and this piecing together of the puzzle will only become more important and complex in the future, requiring a new quality of collaboration and joint action. There is the issue, too, of the enormous costs and legal risks of investigative journalism and of investigation more broadly.

If journalists and activists and campaigners are going to work together, then some basic ground rules need to be established. For one, evidence should be fundamental for advocates and activists, as well as for journalists, if the starting point is a commitment to uncover and disseminate the truth.

Cooperation should be transparent, both between journalists and civil society, and with audiences and other constituencies about the nature and extent of that cooperation, as well as how the work is funded.[103]

Cooperation depends upon mutual independence – if collaboration was portrayed on a Venn diagram, the overlap between parties to a shared investigation would constitute a thin sliver; each has to have its own staff, and legal, security, and risk support, – and clear understanding of potential conflicts of interest.

In conclusion, it would be a mistake to believe that journalists and advocates/activists can remain unchanged by this cooperation – by understanding we're in a battle, we have to act politically (not politicise our work), what we can unite around, despite our differences. As journalism professor Jay Rosen wrote in late 2016 about prospects for the American press under Trump, 'staying independent does not mean standing alone' (Rosen 2016).

When I engineered a partnership with ICIJ in 2011, a mere six years or so ago, it was seen as controversial by some inside the BBC. Since then, however, the BBC has partnered with ICIJ and other journalistic organisations on many occasions. I think the idea of what is in effect at its heart a more systematic sharing of data and evidence – so it can be used in more varied ways – may be controversial now, and some will continue to hold their noses and it will continue to be controversial. But should it be in the future?

As the writer and thinker William Gibson put it, 'The future is already here, it is just not evenly distributed.'

---

[103] Funding issues, of course, are critically important but beyond the scope of this paper. Although there are many funding models, some non-profit journalism organisations are looking at new business models which raise a whole new set of questions.

6

Collaborative Journalism and the Law in the UK

Jan Clements

Collaborative journalism takes many forms. An explosion of high-profile data journalism projects has brought together a wide range of news publishers across borders.[104] Multi-organisational and multinational collaboration is no longer an occasional event.[105]

Collaborations are not new but the scale has changed. Journalism is increasingly globalised, and collaborations often include hundreds of journalists in different jurisdictions dealing with highly sensitive data – which raises a number of fresh legal considerations. It's sensible therefore, as the first step in any collaboration, to talk to your lawyer.

These projects have developed as journalists gain access to quantities of data that can only be analysed with the input of huge technical resources and time. New capabilities such as crowdsourcing changed news organisation's working models – 'scoops' have given way to an open-source model. An early example resulted from the acquisition and publication by the *Daily Telegraph* of leaked official data it had purchased, which showed abuses of the MPs' expenses system. It raised questions about what is ethical newsgathering and the extent to which that conduct is within the law. The data required swift analysis:

> *The Daily Telegraph may have had a team of 25 journalists working on the MPs' expenses but within 10 minutes of the launch on Thursday afternoon of the Guardian's crowdsourcing application to examine them there were 323 people, almost all outside the Guardian, doing the same task. (Guardian, 18 June 2009)*

---

[104] Wikileaks diplomatic cables amounted to 1.7 gigabytes; HSBC 3.3; Lux Tax files 4; Wikileaks Afghanistan protocols 1.4; Panama Papers 2.3 terabytes.
[105] Anika Gupta, 'Bringing Collaborative Journalism to the Issue of International Migration: An Interview about the 19 Million Hackathon'. *Media Fields Journal* 12, 'Media and Migration'.

The more open approach, at least to partners in a project, means that complex agreements are reached and mostly adhered to without a great deal of legal input. In fact, overdependence on lawyers at the outset can alienate sources and give the impression that the publisher is 'driven by fear rather than conviction and determination'.[106]

In projects involving leaked sensitive information it may be inappropriate to set out all of the terms and conditions in formal written contracts and non-disclosure agreements. Trust forms the basis of such collaborations as it is understood that any partner who fails to comply with the agreement will not be invited into the next collaboration. As one journalist put it, 'it's like a golf club; if you break the rules you don't get any more games'.[107] Yet, somehow clear rules must be agreed and roles defined by the partners to a collaborative project. This cannot always be done remotely. Organisations like ICIJ[108] recommend at least one face-to-face meeting at the outset in order to ensure that partners trust each other and understand what is expected. Collaboration needs patience, tact, and discipline, qualities not found in every journalist or editor.

Legal documents have their place, but it seems unlikely that a court would enforce a contract or written agreement covering the publication of, say, leaked material that it would regard as 'tainted with illegality'.[109] This is a matter of ongoing debate; should newsgatherers have the protection of a general defence based on public interest and if so, how can that be given and properly circumscribed? Would it lead to journalists considering themselves somehow 'above the law'? On the other hand, should well-managed, proportionate conduct in the public interest be considered criminal or tortious in the first place (Millar and Scott 2016)?

Each publisher will be liable for its own publication and will have to take its own advice. If possible the allocation of liability for joint projects should be clarified in writing. Shared resources can result in shared responsibility and shared damage to reputation, sometimes unexpectedly.

The McAlpine case illustrates how problems can arise – Angus Stickler, an award-winning former BBC journalist then employed by the Bureau of Investigative Journalism (TBIJ), was seconded by TBIJ to the BBC to work

---

[106] 'Rather than report the story quickly and aggressively, the *Washington Post* had assembled a large team of lawyers who were making all kinds of demands and issuing all sorts of dire warnings. To the source, this signalled that the *Post*, handed what he believed was an unprecedented journalistic opportunity, was being driven by fear rather than conviction and determination.' (Greenwald 2014: 18).

[107] Interview with Jan Clements.

[108] https://www.icij.org/blog/2015/02/behind-scenes-icijs-biggest-ever-collaboration

[109] Patel v Mirza Supreme Court 2016 UKSC 42.

on a paedophile abuse story as he had researched similar stories in the past. In 2012, the BBC's *Newsnight* programme ran the story which consisted of an interview with a man who described the way he was abused as child by someone he understood to be a senior Tory figure. The abuser was not named in the *Newsnight* programme but after it was broadcast individuals on social media identified Lord McAlpine as the alleged culprit. He later sued the BBC and a number of people who had tweeted about him.

The reputational damage to the BBC and the Bureau was serious and several people resigned afterwards, including the journalist and Iain Overton, managing editor of TBIJ. There was no written agreement to set out that the reporter was on loan from TBIJ and working for the BBC. TBIJ had not expected to be drawn into a libel action resulting from the *Newsnight* broadcast. In its apology its trustees expressed regret that Stickler had been seconded without TBIJ retaining editorial control.[110]

Working Principles and Contracts

The terms of an editorial contract would include details of ownership of original material, distribution, publication dates, copyright and other rights, fees, any share of profits from republication, and whether exclusivity is granted. It defines who has editorial control on a day-to-day basis and final editorial control. A joint press strategy may be agreed. The agreement may specify that the work must meet relevant professional standards in compliance with editorial codes. It may also include indemnities for legal actions such as defamation, breach of contract, contempt of court, or at least that the parties will ensure insofar as it is within their knowledge, information, and belief that the work will not give rise to such risks. If these are set out in writing, albeit not a formal contract, they would have legal weight.

Who will be party to the collaboration? Due diligence in these circumstances requires that the initiators of the project should consider the aims and methods of potential partners. The editorial approach of the news organisation must be the right match. Marina Walker, Deputy Director of ICIJ, reportedly told Margaret Sullivan of the *New York Times* (*NYT*) that ICIJ chose not to approach the *NYT* about Panama Papers as in the past the

---

[110] https://www.thebureauinvestigates.com/blog/2012-11-15/statement-from-the-bureaus-trustees-regarding-lord-mcalpine. Angus Stickler resigned and Iain Overton resigned as Managing Editor of TBIJ.

New York Times editors had not shown interest in ICIJ collaborations and that there was a potential 'culture clash'. ICIJ collaborations reject the idea of one party holding the scoop, depending on 'the idea of sharing all material, not keeping anything exclusive and agreeing to observe embargoes for when material would be published'.[111]

Collaborative partners often rely on working practices such as FinanceUncovered's 'Working Together Guidance' which sets out various principles and standards, rather than formal contracts. The paperwork is usually short. When Jill Abramson and Dean Baquet of the *NYT* slipped into the *Guardian*'s London office to discuss collaborating on the Snowden material, the *Guardian* simply had 14 conditions for the project, which were set out on a single sheet of A4 (Harding 2016: 189).

If possible, face-to-face meetings enable partners to build mutual trust and readiness to share information.[112] Multi-encrypted access to hubs to facilitate international cooperation may be required. Each project is different, but in most cases, once ground rules are agreed, each news outlet and staff gets on with its own data analysis.

Partners also need to agree how to describe and to credit the published material. Other parts of the project may be more loosely defined. The details may be set out in various ways – informally in emails, working guidelines, a memorandum of understanding, or a formal contract. Agreement must be reached on embargoes, publishing times and places. How far will proposed material be shared for advance approval, for example if any of the partners have expertise or information that is essential knowledge for pre-publication checks? There is a fine line between checking the facts and 'copy approval', which is anathema to most news organisations that resist relinquishing editorial control. This must be handled extremely carefully.

What happens if the agreement is breached? It may be that trust will have gone and the offending partner will not be included in a future collaboration. Or it may mean that everyone is forced to publish earlier than expected, as in 2010 when Al Jazeera rushed out material from Wikileaks before other partners and Wikileaks tweeted:

> *22 Oct 2010 – Al Jazeera have broken our embargo by 30 minutes. We release everyone from their Iraq War Logs embargoes.*[113]

---

[111] Marina Walker quoted in Sullivan, 'Panama Papers: Why No Big Splash?', https://publiceditor.blogs.nytimes.com/2016/04/04/why-no-big-splash-for-panama-papers/

[112] Obermaier and Obermayer 2017: 85. https://eic.network/blog/making-a-network

[113] https://twitter.com/wikileaks/status/28438570865

Journalistic Privilege

The need to protect the press's role as a 'public watchdog' has long been recognised by the courts: 'the proper functioning of a modern participatory democracy requires that the media be free, active, professional and enquiring … the need for any restriction on that freedom to be proportionate and no more than is necessary to promote the legitimate object of the restriction.'[114] The courts have recognised the 'safety valve of investigative journalism',[115] but what is the scope of that protection?

Collaborations often involve third-sector non-profit organisations with particular expertise such as Greenpeace or Global Witness. Their contribution is usually on a non-commercial basis, although sometimes more like the conventional 'freelance-brings-in-story' model which is dealt in the same way as other freelance journalists. Developing case law suggests that similar journalistic freedoms should apply to NGOs or academics or anyone – such as citizen journalists – who acts as 'watchdog' to publish information on issues of public interest.[116]

Access to information is crucial: 'the press cannot expose that of which it is denied knowledge' (R v Shayler [2001] EWCA Crim 1977) and perhaps it is no coincidence that a collaborative approach developed around freedom of information issues. In a global system where data are often held secretively, on an increasingly large scale 'everyone around the world wants to know what people in power are doing. They want a say in decisions made in their name and with their money', as investigative journalist Heather Brooke (2012) put it.

Mapping that information, and crowdsourcing it, has resulted in a collective form of data journalism. Alaveteli.org allows citizens to request information using freedom of information legislation and for the replies to be recorded for all to see on the website. Historical requests and any correspondences are placed online, acting as 'a useful tool for citizens and as an advocacy tool for right-to-know campaigners'. Using Alaveteli, freedom of information websites have been set up around the world, including Whatdotheyknow.com in the UK. Other projects include Afrileaks, Securedrop, and platforms for mapping corruption and violence such as Ushahidi.com in Kenya.[117]

---

[114] McCartan Turkington Breen v Times 2001 2 AC 277.

[115] R v CCC ex p Bright, Alton, Rusbridger QBD 21 Jul 2000.

[116] Kennedy v Charity Commission 2014 UKSC 20.

[117] http://blog.transparency.org/2013/05/02/ushahidi-an-introduction-to-anti-corruption-mapping/; https://www.ushahidi.com/about.

In Kennedy v Charity Commission the Supreme Court suggested that journalistic freedoms should also apply to NGOs, academics, and anyone else who acts as 'watchdog' to raise issues of public interest. Beny Steinmetz, mining billionaire,[118] sought information from non-profit organisation Global Witness (GW), claiming he was entitled to do so under the Data Protection Act 1998. His argument was that this was personal data and GW was a campaigning organisation, not a news organisation, and should not be entitled to journalistic protection. He failed in his bid as the High Court referred the matter back to the Information Commissioner, who reviewed his earlier decision and accepted the information held by GW was protected under section 32 of the Data Protection Act as journalistic material.

Involvement in the journalistic project should be clearly defined. It is important that secure systems are devised to protect the journalistic material. Those involved in the project – professional journalists or not – may face attempts to search and seize the material from them (e.g. under the Police and Criminal Evidence Act 1984 or Schedule 7 of the Terrorism Act) and will need to assert the fact that they are dealing with journalistic material when challenged by authorities, so that rights under Article 10 Freedom of Expression may be taken into account. These issues arose in the case of R (oao) David Miranda v Home Secretary and Commissioner of Metropolitan Police.[119]

Legal Privilege

Journalists can collaborate on many issues but they are constrained in the extent of their ability to share legal advice. Legal advice privilege is a category of privilege attached to confidential communications between clients and their lawyers during the 'ordinary course of (the client's) business'. If editorial organisations swap and share legal advice, they will lose the protection of 'privilege', i.e. the right to keep legal advice confidential.

Each news publisher should take its own legal advice as each organisation is separately liable. In-house legal counsel can advise its internal 'client team', but cannot advise third parties without risking the loss of legal professional privilege. In the case of legal advice privilege, the protection from disclosure may be lost if the client news organisation shares with a non-lawyer third

---

[118] https://www.globalwitness.org/en/archive/information-commissioner-throws-out-beny-steinmetz-complaint-against-global-witness
[119] R (David Miranda) and Secretary of State for Home Dept and Commissioner of Met Police et al. C1/2014/0607 19/01/2016, 61–7.

party the confidential legal advice received from a lawyer. Without privilege, the legal advice would lose the protection of confidentiality and may have to be disclosed in litigation. This exposure could be very damaging.

On the other hand, it is sometimes possible for lawyers from different organisations to talk to each other about the legal issues and to share common interest privilege. However, cross-jurisdictional issues may make this difficult.

Partners in a collaborative project may decide to seek joint legal advice on particular issues where there is a common interest. However, this can be cumbersome in news publishing, where quick and nimble responses to legal issues are needed. While shared advice at the outset might be helpful, it is unlikely to work for day-to-day editorial legal issues, particularly in a large-scale project.

If non-lawyers in the project give legal advice – even if they are professionals such as accountants – this will not be treated by the court as confidential and privileged legal advice.[120] (This short chapter should not be regarded as legal advice; it can only highlight the issues that arise in collaborative projects in the context of UK law.)

Information Security and Data Protection

Newsgathering practices involve processing personal data, and the Information Commissioner's Office has published useful guidance regarding media's obligations under the Data Protection Act (DPA)1998.[121] Note, that it is just guidance and not of statutory weight.

One of the key data protection principles is to keep data secure. It is also a central concern for collaborators in a project that involves leaked, highly sensitive material.

Security needs and legal issues often overlap. The sharing of huge amounts of leaked data requires joint agreement about security, analytical effort, and shared resources. Technical skills involving encryption programmes and solid security measures are needed.[13] The protection of personal data is essential to protect sources and the mass of personal data that is yet to be explored.

---

[120] See R (oao) Prudential v Special Commissioner on Income Tax 2013. https://www.supremecourt.uk/cases/docs/uksc-2010-0215-judgment.pdf, p. 71.

[121] https://ico.org.uk/media/for-organisations/documents/1552/data-protection-and-journalism-media-guidance.pdf

Access to personal data should be controlled and limited to those with specific roles. The more sensitive the data, the more restricted the access needs to be. These measures will not only protect the source material for journalistic reasons but will also help to meet the legal requirements of the 7th Data Protection Principle set out in Schedule 1 of the DPA 1998 to keep personal data secure. Security of personal data is one of the elements of data protection law that is not made exempt by section 32 of the Act, the journalistic exemption.

The sharing and processing of personal data in these collaborative projects would be unlawful if the data processing was not for a journalistic purpose.[122] In order to take advantage of the journalistic exemption set out in section 32 of DPA the following requirements must be met: the processing of personal information must take place with a view to publication; the processor must reasonably believe that publication would be in the public interest and also believe that compliance with the DPA (such as ceasing to deal with the data) would be incompatible with the journalistic purpose.[123]

If all of the section 32 requirements are met, the data processing is exempt from key provisions of the DPA 1998 such as a subject access request, or the right of the subject to prevent processing or require the data to be erased or destroyed. However, until they are examined and checked it may be difficult to distinguish personal data that should be published in the public interest from the personal data that do not meet that standard.

Questions arise about how to interrogate the database and how to deal with any personal data in a large data dump that is not going to be published. The public interest should be considered at each stage, for example: on receipt of the information and before interrogating the database; on deciding which aspects or which individuals to investigate; and on deciding whether the story is of sufficient public interest to justify publication. A fishing expedition is not justified;[124] there should be some idea of alleged suspected wrongdoing before even exploring the data. Editorial codes provide helpful guidance on public interest.[125]

Similarly, actions for breach of privacy and breach of confidence may be defeated if the journalistic investigation and publication is in the public interest. What is in the public interest may range from exposing hypocrisy

---

[122] It may be possible to argue another exemption – prevention and detection of crime – but it is a narrow exemption.
[123] http://www.legislation.gov.uk/ukpga/1998/29/section/32
[124] See PCC adjudication on Vince Cable complaint 2011.
[125] https://www.ipso.co.uk/editors-code-of-practice

to exposing criminal wrongdoing.[126] However, there is a public interest in freedom of expression itself, as recognised in the DPA 1998 and in media guidance published by the Information Commissioner.[127]

The question of public interest is vital. Editorial and legal interests collide – the greater the public interest, the greater the impact of a story and the more likely that the publisher can rely on it as a defence to legal actions such as breach of data protection, breach of confidence and privacy actions, as well as defamation.

The public interest is defined differently in different legal and regulatory contexts. It may be easier to determine what is not in the public interest such as 'the most vapid tittle-tattle about the activities of footballers' wives and girlfriends interests large sections of the public but no-one could claim any real public interest in our being told all about it' – as Baroness Hale told the House of Lords in the case of Jameel and others.[128]

There are not many statutory definitions. Public Interest Disclosure Act 1998 (protecting whistleblowers) sets out various factors and the defence set out for public interest journalism in section 4 of the Defamation Act 2013 is useful.[129] The regulatory codes of the old Press Complaints Commission now IPSO, Ofcom, BBC, and other news organisations are useful references.

In breach of confidence the public interest in, for example, exposing wrongdoing, provides a 'limiting principle' that amounts to a defence for a breach. In an action for misuse of private information, the public interest forms a key part of the ultimate balancing exercise. The public interest in journalism and the right to freedom of expression in Article 10 ECHR may have to give way to competing private or public interests.

The DPP Guidelines for Prosecutors on Assessing the Public Interest in cases affecting the media (CPS 2012) sets out criteria for prosecutors to consider whether it is in the public interest to pursue actions against the media. There is no single definition and there is no generalised public interest defence that the press can rely on universally.

The question of whether apparently unlawful newsgathering is nonetheless justified in the public interest can be a matter of perspective. The same is true of unlawful whistleblowing. In hard cases, it seems likely

---

[126] E.g. see IPSO code https://www.ipso.co.uk/editors-code-of-practice/#ThePublicInterest and s4 Defamation Act 2013.

[127] https://ico.org.uk/media/for-organisations/documents/1552/data-protection-and-journalism-media-guidance.pdf

[128] (Respondents) v Wall Street Journal Europe (Jameel, 147). http://www.5rb.com/wp-content/uploads/2013/10/Jameel-v-Wall-Street-Journal-HL-11-Oct-2006.pdf

[129] http://www.legislation.gov.uk/ukpga/2013/26/section/4/enacted

that the courts will still often have to decide. A generic public interest defence could make a significant difference (Millar and Scott 2016).[130]

Commenting on the government decision to drop the Derek Pasquill prosecution – he leaked info to journalists about renditions by USA – led the *Observer* newspaper to note the 'emerging view among some law lords that [the] public interest should be taken into account'.[131]

Accuracy and Responsible Journalism

The first editorial step is to verify that the data is 'authentic and socially relevant'. As Denis Miller in The Conversation points out, journalism is more than an information dump. 'Journalism requires truth-telling. Verifying that material is genuine then publishing it in a way that is accurate as to plain facts and context'.[132]

Verification is not always easy, and sometimes seems impossible when huge quantities of data are leaked. Collaborations can assist. Projects such as Wikileaks, Snowden, and Panama Papers bring together skilled technicians to devise sophisticated data search tools as well as the traditional investigatory tools: checking hundreds of pages of files against material from other investigations or publicly available court documents and other information in public databases to authenticate and corroborate the information (Obermaier and Obermayer 2017: 48–9).

These checks are essential for obvious journalistic reasons but also to be able to avoid legal complaints and to defend a libel action. Libel risks arise in the context of any publication and this article only considers the areas that might impact or be affected by the fact that the project is a collaborative one.

The most likely libel defences for projects of this kind are: truth (section 2 Defamation Act 2013) but, more likely, public interest journalism (section 4 Defamation Act 2013). Clearly, the journalistic project involves seeking the truth – checking facts, seeking corroboration, and getting the strongest evidence possible to show the truth of any allegations. But to rely on this

---

[130] See also defence of 'necessity' raised in the case of Katharine Gun, translator at GCHQ, who was prosecuted under section 1 of the Official Secrets Act 1989 after disclosing that the US National Security Agency had requested British assistance in conducting surveillance on other states at UN.

[131] https://www.theguardian.com/commentisfree/2008/jan/13/politics.uk

[132] http://theconversation.com/wikileaks-journalism-ethics-and-the-digital-age-what-did-we-learn-28262, 1 July 2014.

defence alone contains risks, not least that is difficult to predict what evidence might be admissible at a future libel trial.

Globalisation has impacted on us all, and journalists are increasingly investigating global issues such as offshore tax avoidance. Cross-border collaborations include Offshore Secrets, Luxembourg Tax Files, and HSBC Files, and organisations like ICIJ have since 1997 coordinated many joint investigations into issues such as global tobacco trafficking, international trade in body parts, and the role of the World Bank. As FinanceUncovered (formerly Tax Justice Network) puts it, collaboration is necessary to follow the 'global financial flows'.[133] It is through such cross-border collaboration that evidence can be put together and corroborated in order to try to sustain a defence of truth, under section 1 of the Defamation Act.

Section 4 of the Defamation Act provides a defence where it can be shown that the publication 'was or formed part of a statement on a matter of public interest'; and that the defendant reasonably assessed the circumstances of the case, including what steps were taken to verify the information, how reliable the source was, whether the allegations were put to the subject of the story for a response, and whether the gist of their side of the story was included in the publication.

In a collaborative context, there will need to be some discussion about how to handle this process – who will make the approaches for comment and will this trigger an application for an injunction in breach of confidence? Should each partner make their own approaches, or will responses be shared?

The collaboration may involve dividing stories between journalists in different jurisdictions. The German journalists Bastian Obermayer and Frederik Obermaier were overwhelmed by the huge quantity of data in the Panama Papers and said,[134]

we must naturally focus our attention on major German scoops. At the same time we don't want the [other] stories to be ignored or lost in countries where they might be of interest. That is a compelling argument for a large-scale international collaboration of the kind we participated in during Offshore Secrets, the Luxembourg Tax Files and the HSBC files.

---

[133] http://www.financeuncovered.org
[134] Obermaier, F. and B. Obermayer. 2017. *The Panama Papers: Breaking the Story of How the Rich and Powerful Hide their Money.* London: Oneworld

Legal Threats

Collaboration between news publishers can create a feeling – and a reality – of safety in numbers. If there are threats to gag publication in one jurisdiction the story can appear in another part of the world. In response to the Wikileaks diplomatic cables story, Mastercard took the Wikileaks site offline for a time, by blocking Wikileaks' fundraising.[135] But this could not prevent further publication by the *New York Times*, the *Guardian*, *Le Monde*, *El País*, and *Der Spiegel* too. This illustrates the power of collaboration versus the traditional journalistic 'exclusive'; sometimes cooperation provides a better legal card to play.

When *Guardian* journalist David Leigh and lawyers met HSBC after they sent the *Guardian* threatening legal letters, he told them, 'if they injuncted us it would merely increase ICIJ coverage in the US and other jurisdictions, which they could not stop. This is an immensely useful legal shield.'

Similarly, the *New York Times* responded to the US government that their appeals to dissuade them from publishing Snowden material were useless as the *Guardian* in London also had the material to publish.

Other questions arise about arbitrage: jurisdiction and where to publish or who should publish first. Significant differences in legal and political approaches to the right to freedom of expression and questions of national security influence decisions about where to publish and this is one reason why the Snowden leaks were first published in US. Snowden allegations concerned the US National Security Agency and the GCHQ in UK, and the *Guardian* lawyers needed to consider the possible criminal law risks under the Official Secrets Act 1989 and also the civil risks of a pre-publication injunction. Gill Phillips, Director of Editorial Legal Services at the *Guardian* said:

> *What you're really looking at is making sure you can get the story out. This comes into focus when you are deciding whether you should put the key allegations to the relevant parties before publication, as that can tip them off and give them a chance to get into court. You want to avoid that if you can.*[136]

She points out that the First Amendment and the Pentagon Papers case mean that a pre-publication injunction is highly unlikely to be sought in

---

[135] http://news.nationalpost.com/news/wikileaks-suspending-publication-to-focus-on-fundraising-survival

[136] http://www.inhouselawyer.co.uk/index.php/mag-feature/legal-pathway-to-the-story-of-the-century

the US as often as in the UK. US newspapers feel freer to contact parties before publication and as a consequence, the US government was much more willing to engage in discussions about the Snowden material.

Both governments sought the return of the material, but the *New York Times* was able to 'test' the Snowden material with the Pentagon before publication. And despite the fact that MI5 officers required the *Guardian* to destroy its computer hard drive, this became a largely symbolic act as the data were also held by other journalists in different jurisdictions.[137] And the key material had been published. If things are going to happen in America come what may, it's a bit pointless trying to close things down in the UK.

The powers of the police and other authorities to seize journalistic material are limited in statute and by Article 10 of the ECHR. Collaborators should be aware of the potential criminal offences of failing to disclose information under section 19 and section 38B of the Terrorism Act 2000: where a person fails to provide information regarding terrorist activities to police, this conflicts with the journalistic obligation to protect source but will also raise ethical considerations if the source is engaged in extremist action. The consent of the Director of Public Prosecutions (DPP) is required for a prosecution for either offence and if so, the DPP guidance on prosecuting the media should come into play. There is a defence of 'reasonable excuse' which might cover the protection of sources; the burden of proof is on the defence.

There are various other statutory powers to compel the production of documents or providing information, such as section 17 of the Financial Services & Markets Act 2000, which may require production of documents where the investigator 'reasonably considers the production ... to be relevant to the purposes of an ongoing investigation'. Failure to comply without reasonable excuse can be treated as though in contempt. Once again, there is a potential defence of 'reasonable excuse' which has not yet been tested in court in relation to journalism. But the court would be obliged to conduct a balancing act over whether compulsory disclosure is a necessary and proportionate restriction on newsgathering freedom.[138]

---

[137] https://www.theguardian.com/world/2013/aug/20/nsa-snowden-files-drives-destroyed-london. David Leigh interview.

[138] Other compulsory powers under s2 Criminal Justice Act 1987; s62 Serious Organised Crime and Policing Act 2005.

Sources and Others

'Who is the source?' is an important question, given the ethical and legal obligation to preserve their confidentiality. Information brokers are not regarded as 'sources' to which the classic journalistic obligations apply and they do not seek confidentiality.[29] The duties one owes to such brokers are partly contractual, partly about dealing fairly in a more general way. ICIJ has frequently taken the precaution of not identifying its source to any 'partners'. A collaborative group needs to discuss and decide who owns the relationship with source and whether joint approaches to the source are viable.

The courts recognise that confidential journalistic sources require protection. Goodwin v UK (ECtHR 1996 [28]) is a powerful affirmation of source protection and section 10 of the Contempt of Court Act 1981 gives qualified protection to sources. The protection goes further than just the identity of sources; it extends to journalistic information and materials that have not been published.[139]

The Human Rights Act 1998 requires that any legal powers used to force disclosure should be understood and given effect to in a way which is compatible with the presumptive Convention right to protect a source.

In a recommendation[140] adopted by the Committee of Ministers of the Council of Europe on 8 March 2000, on the right of journalists not to disclose sources of information, journalists are defined as those regularly or professional engaged in the collection and dissemination of information to the public. Principle 2 calls for member states to extend this protection to others who, through professional relations with journalists, acquire knowledge identifying a source.[141] Disclosure should be compelled only if there exists 'an overriding requirement in the public interest and if circumstances are of a sufficiently vital and serious nature'.

Article 10 clearly extends to other journalistic material, not just the identity of sources. In R v Central Criminal Court ex parte Bright, Alton and Rusbridger [2001] the court said 'compelling evidence is normally needed to demonstrate that the public interest would be served by such proceedings' for the seizure of working papers.

---

[139] X LTD v MORGAN-GRAMPIAN (PUBLISHERS) LTD: HL 1990, 51–3. http://swarb.co.uk/x-ltd-v-morgan-grampian-publishers-ltd-hl-1990

[140] https://www.coe.int/en/web/freedom-expression/committee-of-ministers-adopted-texts/-/asset_publisher/aDXmrol0vvsU/content/recommendation-no-r-2000-7-of-the-committee-of-ministers-to-member-states-on-the-right-of-journalists-not-to-disclose-their-sources-of-information?_101_INSTANCE_aDXmrol0vvsU_viewMode=view

[141] 'Source' is widely defined as anyone giving information to a journalist.

Care should be taken about who holds material and how secure it is, given potential police powers to search and seize material under PACE 1984.[142] The PACE 1984 Schedule 1 scheme, section 9 'journalistic material' provides some protection to material acquired or created for the purpose of journalism, including material received from someone who intends that it shall be used by the recipient for purposes of journalism, and would cover documents or data unsolicited and received from anonymous sources. However, once material moves out of the possession of the person who acquired or created it for purposes of journalism, it is no longer protected as journalistic material.[143]

Awareness of security issues is vital. When the German journalists from the Panama Papers investigation travelled to Washington they made sure that they were not in the position to grant anyone access to the data. They did not have with them the 40-character password for the most secure information and only later sent it to the ICIJ once back in Germany (Obermaier and Obermayer 2017).

Other important ethical or legal issues arise about the protection of third parties who are unwittingly involved. For example, in the Wikileaks diplomatic cables story (Cablegate) the *Guardian* redacted details that might identify activists and informants who may have suffered reprisals.[144]

In conclusion, there are few, if any, current legal precedents for what happens when agreements break down, promises are broken, or people and organisations behave badly in order to protect their own interests in the collaborative project. But there have been situations that indicate that one should not view collaborative journalism with rosy spectacles. Even at the best of times, there will be stresses and strains around personal and organisational self-interest – who 'owns' the story, has someone taken credit for all of the work unfairly, is one news organisation promoting its own brand without crediting others?

With the best of intentions things go wrong – more often than not, accidentally. In relation to Cablegate, a date and time were set for publication, 21.30GMT Sunday 28 November, but a 'rogue copy' of *Der Spiegel* went on sale by mistake at Basel station in Switzerland at 11.30 am that day. Heather Brooke (2012) describes the panic: 'The carefully constructed embargo was trashed and the papers rushed forward their online publication. The *Guardian*'s splash went online at 6.13pm.'

---

[142] https://www.legislation.gov.uk/ukpga/1984/60/contents (Accessed 9 Oct. 2017)
[143] S13 (2) PACE 1984.
[144] http://www.bbc.co.uk/news/technology-37165230

Surreal situations can arise such as when Julian Assange, distressed at the *New York Times* publishing a critical account of him, refused to give them the Wikileaks data. The *New York Times* got hold of the information from another source, but Assange believed the *Guardian* may have given them the data. This led to Assange and his lawyers bursting into the editor, Alan Rusbridger's office and threatening to take action for breaching an embargo. The world's best-known publisher of leaked material was complaining about the information he had obtained being leaked without his permission.

The ethos of collaboration contrasts with the traditional focus on exclusive scoops. While each partner may have its own scoops, resources are shared and timetables agreed amongst the partners. In a world where newspapers have shrinking resources, this kind of collaboration seems to be the way forward. Clarity is essential about shared responsibilities, and the relationship between non-profit organisations and traditional news organisations, preferably in writing. Careful consideration should be given to the different approaches to freedom of expression in different jurisdictions and the potential advantages to the publications.

New editorial and legal models are evolving to cope with a world in which print and online media are struggling to survive. There are fewer resources for investigations. A coalition of journalists, IT experts, data analysts, and NGOs provides the best way to unpick and investigate the mass of data about global issues. As new journalistic projects develop, so lawyers must focus on how best to protect their editorial clients.

Conclusions

Richard Sambrook

Collaboration strengthens journalism and supports investigation at a time when serious accountability reporting is under pressure from many directions.

There is now a strong narrative around the failure of much journalism to adapt to the technological era or to adequately adapt to fast changing social, political, and business circumstances. The increasingly widespread cries of 'fake news' and falling trust levels in media threaten to undermine the legitimacy and effectiveness of serious reporting. The need for those concerned with accountability journalism to collaborate and support each other has never been greater. Today, newsrooms are faced daily with the rise of opinion overshadowing evidence, the huge resources now placed behind corporate and political public relations and spin, and the increasing complexity of how data and information are managed across new platforms and territories – with bots gaming people's news feeds in ways they cannot hope to understand.

The case studies discussed here indicate how collaboration between journalists can bring resources, expertise, and institutional strength to bear on increasingly complex stories in ways which would otherwise not be possible. In that sense, these collaborations point forward to a new approach to investigative journalism, adapting to political, social, and commercial pressures, which might otherwise defeat conventional methods. Those concerned with high-quality, verified, evidence-led journalism, which holds the powerful to account, must work together if it is to flourish in these new circumstances.

Collaboration has in one sense been part of journalism's history since it began to industrialise in the 19th century. However, the age of data and the technology that is now redefining communications means there are new opportunities for cooperation.

The scale of data being leaked is beyond the capabilities of most conventional news organisations to handle on their own. Collaboration allows them to pool resources and expertise to investigate issues of public significance which, without such collaboration, would go unreported.

As politics, business, trade, and, indeed, crime all develop into transnational activities it is essential that journalism and those concerned with public accountability similarly respond. The need for news organisations to raise their sights beyond national boundaries and to raise their skills to engage with the highly developed systems of financial technology or internet-enabled crime is now acute. The overall concept of public accountability – and, in particular, the important journalism about it – increasingly cannot and should not be narrowly confined by mere geographic boundaries.

Similarly, journalists should stop thinking they can always 'go it alone'. International accountability is an issue for lawyers, economists, politicians and lobbyists, scientists, health care professionals, academics, accountancy, business and finance professionals, and more. In a modern approach to accountability journalism, newsrooms should seek to partner and collaborate outside their profession as widely as possible, being open to the expertise of others.

This includes across the boundaries between activism and journalism. There are common interests which may allow fruitful collaboration between these different sectors. And, as the Greenpeace case example shows, investigative journalism is increasingly being seen as an activist tool. It is important to manage the boundaries clearly and transparently but it seems likely a more systematic sharing of data and evidence between different sectors is likely and desirable in future if journalism is to maintain its watchdog role in the new international environment.

But the risk of journalism being captured by politics remains real. It is fashionable in the age of digital plenty to eschew traditional notions of objectivity and impartiality. Yet to do so and 'choose sides' rather than be led by evidence diminishes journalism. Evidence-led journalism put through the editorial discipline of objectivity is harder work than reporting with a predetermined affiliation – and more powerful for it. Data provide major new opportunities for evidence-based reporting – but all data require interpretation and collaborators need to be wary of partners with agendas.

The opportunities afforded by collaboration must not negate the ethical responsibilities of news organisations in relation to leaked data, including interrogating the motivation behind leaks, protection of sources, avoidance of harm, or identifying what lies in the public interest, as opposed to what might simply interest the public.

There are differences of kind between different data leaks. For example, many would argue that Julian Assange and Wikileaks have revealed political motives; that there is a legitimate debate about the public interest of Edward Snowden revealing the scale of secret surveillance set against the potential damage to national interests, and the Panama Papers which encompassed the innocent and legal as well as more suspect financial activities. News organisations in different countries, with different attitudes towards, and legal frameworks around, public information inevitably view these ethical questions differently. Collaborations make already complex legal and ethical issues more difficult – and, given the scale of such leaks, the onus on getting those judgements right even greater.

The rise in pan-national collaboration also reveals something about the state of the news industry. With business models disrupted by digital platforms, many organisations, once regarded as mighty news institutions, are struggling to get by or to field the scale of resources required for long and complex investigations. At the same time, there has been a rise in small start-up organisations – some commercial, some non-profit – seeking to establish and differentiate themselves in a crowded market. These two groups are often conceived as in conflict with one another – the start-up insurgency seeking to undermine big legacy media. In truth, they may often need each other in the new communication environment. Major organisations still have an institutional weight and broad audience reach which newcomers lack. Equally, new players often have technical skills and market nimbleness, and attract a younger audience in ways the major players struggle to achieve.

Where they come together – in pursuing global accountability – they can complement and learn from each other. Big media can provide scale, reach, and institutional strength; smaller organisations can provide new perspectives, new skills, and new audiences.

The arguments made by the contributors to this study show how some parts of the news community are beginning to recognise these opportunities and develop approaches to pursuing new forms of collaboration for investigative journalism. But there is much further to go and there are risks.

This is an area which is dynamic and evolving rapidly. However, from the contributions here, and the discussions which underlie them, it is clear a specific set of factors contributes to the success of such partnerships. It's our hope these may assist others in embarking on collaborative projects and therefore support stronger international investigations in the future.

These factors include:

- Trust building between different organisations, usually from a newsroom level upwards, initially. Newsroom staff find the benefits of collaboration easier to identify than senior executives, who may be overly focused on exclusivity or other competitive factors.
- Confidentiality is crucial and needs to be supported by a high level of 'communication hygiene'. By the time a whistleblower has contacted a news organisation their identity may already be compromised. Secure channels of communication – such as 'dropboxes' – need to be set up and publicised and communication hygiene promoted by news organisations across their staff.
- If non-profit organisations are involved in a collaboration, or third-party funders, objectives and success measures need to be agreed in advance together with principles of editorial independence.
- Technology, and the ability to develop and modify software or other technology to suit the needs of a particular project, is crucial. Developers and journalists need to work in an integrated way.
- A neutral partner can play a valuable role in managing tensions and potential conflicts of interest between partners. In the end, one trusted party has to make decisions and hold other partners to account.
- The argument for funding long-term, complex investigations needs to be continually made – not only within news organisations but also to funders seeking to support non-profit journalism. Funding cannot only be by project – non-profit news organisations require core funding as well.

Finally, there is an argument to be made about the social value of investigative journalism – particularly in a pan-national environment. Governments and foundations understand the value of open data and high-quality information and recognise the corrosive effect of corruption and crime on social, economic, and political well-being. And yet the link between free information, public accountability, and serious journalism is one that has to be continually made.

If James T. Hamilton is right (Hamilton 2016), and a dollar spent in investigative journalism can yield hundreds of dollars in social benefits, then the case for high-profile, collaborative accountability reporting should be easily made. Measuring social benefit is complex and difficult, but those concerned with the health of serious journalism and public support for it need to engage with the problem and highlight it. The case studies discussed here – and the approach which delivered them – illustrate that value.

Strong journalism strengthens society. Collaboration strengthens journalism. As Frederik Obermaier put it:

> *I learned that the more you share, the more radically you share, the better the investigation … I learned that I had to share because without sharing such projects (as The Panama Papers) are not possible. The more transparent such projects are, the better it is. Every media outlet benefitted from this project.*[145]

---

[145] Interview with author, Apr. 2017.

Appendix

Workshop Participants

(16 December 2016, Reuters Institute for the Study of Journalism)

Brigitte Alfter, Managing Europe, Journalismfund.eu

Mar Cabra, Head of Data & Research Unit, International Consortium of Investigative Journalists

Jan Clements, Media lawyer and editorial consultant (Former legal adviser at the *Guardian*, she has also published under her former name of Jan Johannes)

Sylke Gruhnwald, Chair of Journalismfund.eu and Reporter

Eliot Higgins, Founder, Bellingcat

Nicolas Kayser-Bril, Co-founder and CEO, Journalism++

Charles Lewis, Founder, The Center for Public Integrity and Professor of Journalism, American University

Javier Moreno Barber, Director, *El País*

Rasmus Kleis Nielsen, Director of Research, Reuters Institute for the Study of Journalism

Rachel Oldroyd, Managing Editor, Bureau of Investigative Journalism

Gerard Ryle, Director, International Consortium of Investigative Journalists

Richard Sambrook, Professor of Journalism, Cardiff University

Ceri Thomas, Director of Public Affairs and Communications, Oxford University (Former editor BBC *Panorama*)

Tom Warren, Investigations Correspondent, BuzzFeed

International Journalism Festival Panel

Anna Babinets, OCCRP

Mar Cabra, ICIJ

Nicolas Kayser-Bril, Journalism++
Stuart Millar, BuzzFeed UK

Interviewees and Other Contributors

David Alandete, Managing Editor, *El País*
Anne Koch, Program Director, Global Investigative Journalism Network
(Former Regional Director, Transparency International)
Frederik Obermaier, *Süddeutsche Zeitung*
Cécile Prieur, *Le Monde*
Alan Rusbridger, Principal of Lady Margaret Hall, Oxford University
(Former Editor of the *Guardian*)
Adam Thomas, Director, European Journalism Centre

Bibliography

All websites cited in this book were last accessed in July/August 2017 unless otherwise stated.

Organisation Websites

Center for Public Integrity: https://www.publicintegrity.org/

European Investigative Collaborations (EIC): https://eic.network

European Journalism Centre (EJC) http://ejc.net

Global Investigative Journalism Network: http://gijn.org

International Consotium for Investigative Journalists (ICIJ): https://www.icij.org

Journalism++: http://www.jplusplus.org

Journalismfund: http://www.journalismfund.eu

Organised crime and corruption project (OCCRP): https://www.occrp.org/en

ProPublica: https://www.propublica.org/

The Bureau for Investigative Journalism (TBIJ): https://www.thebureauinvestigates.com

Transnational Investigative Journalism Methodology: http://www.tijmethodology.com

Collaborative Sites

Laundromat: https://www.occrp.org/en/laundromat/

Migrant Files: http://www.themigrantsfiles.com

Panama Papers: https://panamapapers.icij.org

Paradise Papers: https://projekte.sueddeutsche.de/paradisepapers/politik/the-new-offshore-leak-e969006/

Snowden Files: https://www.theguardian.com/world/series/the-snowden-files

Tennis matchfixing: https://www.buzzfeed.com/heidiblake/the-tennis-racket
The New Arrivals: https://www.theguardian.com/world/series/the-new-arrivals
Wikileaks Iraq Files: https://wikileaks.org/irq/

Books and Journals

Abramo, Claudio W. 2007. 'Brazil: A Portrait of Disparities', *Brazilian Journalism Research*. https://bjr.sbpjor.org.br/bjr/article/download/101/100

Alabiso, Vincent, Kelly Smith Tunney, and Chuck Zoeller, eds. 1998. *FLASH! The Associated Press Covers the World*. New York: Associated Press in association with Harry N. Abrams

Alfter, Brigitte. 2015. 'Journalistik over grænser – håndbog i crossborder journalistik', *Forlaget Ajour* (Forthcoming in German, autumn 2017)

Alfter, Brigitte. 2016. 'Cross-Border Collaborative Journalism: Why Journalists and Scholars Should Talk about an Emerging Method', *Journal of Applied Journalism and Media Studies* 5/2: 297–311

Askehave, Inger, Malene Gram, and Birgitte Norlyk. 2009. 'Culture in a Business Context', in *Meanings and Messages: Intercultural Business Communication*, 7–31. Århus: Academica

BBC. 2017. *Editorial Guidelines*. Section 4. http://www.bbc.co.uk/editorialguidelines/guidelines/impartiality

BBC Academy. 2017. 'Impartiality'. http://www.bbc.co.uk/academy/journalism/article/art20130702112133788

Beckett, C., and J. Ball. 2010. *Wikileaks: News in the Networked Era*. Cambridge: Polity.

Berglez, Peter. 2008. 'What is Global Journalism? Theoretical and Empirical Conceptualisations', *Journalism Studies* 9/6: 845–58

Berglez, Peter. 2013. *Global Journalism: Theory and Practice*. New York: Peter Lang Publishing

Boaden, Helen. 2017. 'In Search of Unbiased Reporting in Light of Brexit, Trump and Other Reporting Challenges in the UK and US', Shorenstein Center on Media, Politics and Public Policy, 13 June. https://shorensteincenter.org/unbiased-reporting-brexit-trump-uk-us

Boltanski, Luc, and Eve Chiapello. 2005. *The New Spirit of Capitalism*. London: Verso

Brooke, Heather. 2012. '*The Revolution will be Digitised*. London: Windmill Books

Burgh, Hugo de, with Paul Bradshaw, Michael Bromley, Mark D'Arcy, Ivor Gaber, Roy Greenslade, Mark Hanna, Chris Horrie, Paul Lashmar, Gavin MacFadyen. 2008. *Investigative Journalism*, 2nd edn. London: Routledge

CPJ. 2017. *The Best Defense: Threats to Journalists' Safety Demand Fresh Approach*. https://cpj.org/reports/2017/02/Best-Defense-Threats-Safety-Journalists-Freelance-Emergencies-Attack-Digital.php

Department of Justice. 2014. 'Second Vice President of Equatorial Guinea Agrees to Relinquish More Than $30 Million of Assets Purchased with Corruption Proceeds', press release 10 Oct., https://www.justice.gov/opa/pr/second-vice-president-equatorial-guinea-agrees-relinquish-more-30-million-assets-purchased

Ebrahim, Margaret. 1996. *Fat Cat Hotel*. Aug. Washington, DC: Center for Public Integrity. https://iw-files.s3.amazonaws.com/documents/pdfs/fat_cat_hotel_1996_08.pdf

Folha de S. Paulo. 2015. 'African Dictator's Son's Sponsorship Becomes Biggest Controversy at Rio's Carnival', 2 Feb., http://www1.folha.uol.com.br/internacional/en/travel/2015/02/1590896-african-dictators-sons-sponsorship-becomes-biggest-controversy-at-rios-carnival.shtml

FRA. 2016. *Violence, Threats and Pressures Against Journalists and Other Media Actors in the EU*. Brussels: EU. fra.europa.eu/sites/default/files/fra_uploads/fra-2016-threats-and-pressures-journalists_en.pdf

GIJN. 2017. 'Global Investigative Journalism Network Impact Page'. http://impact.gijn.org

Global Witness. 2017. 'Undercover in New York'. https://www.globalwitness.org/shadyinc

Greenwald, Glenn. 2014. *No Place to Hide*. New York: Penguin Books.

Guardian. 2017. 'DIY Political Websites: New Force Shaping the General Election Debate', 1 June. https://www.theguardian.com/politics/2017/jun/01/diy-political-websites-new-force-shaping-general-election-debate-canary

Gupta, Anika. 2016. 'Bringing Collaborative Journalism to the Issue of International Migration: An Interview about the 19 Million Hackathon'. *Media Fields Journal* 12, 'Media and Migration'.

Gynnild, Astrid. 2014. 'Journalism Innovation Leads to Innovation Journalism: The Impact of Computational Exploration on Changing Mindsets', *Journalism* 15/6: 713–30

Hamilton, James T. 2016. *Democracy's Detectives: The Economics of Investigative Journalism*. Cambridge, MA: Harvard University Press

Harding, Luke. 2016. *The Snowden Files*. London: Guardian Faber

Hunter, Mark Lee, Luk N. Van Wassenhove, and Maria Besious. 2016. *Power is Everywhere – How Stakeholder-Driven Media Build the Future of Watchdog News.* Fontainebleu: INSEAD Business School, The Stakeholder Media Project. http://www.comminit.com/global/content/power-everywhere

ICIJ. 2010. *Dangers in the Dust: Inside the Global Asbestos Trade.* Washington, DC: Center for Public Integrity. https://www.icij.org/project/dangers-dust

ICIJ. 2016. International Anti Corruption Conference Panel: Journalists and Activists – More Light, More Heat. Panama City, Dec.

ICIJ. 2017. 'Explore the Documents: Luxembourg Leaks Database'. https://www.icij.org/project/luxembourg-leaks/explore-documents-luxembourg-leaks-database

ICIJ. 2017. 'The Panama Papers'. https://panamapapers.icij.org

Jacobs, Jane. 1992. *Systems of Survival.* New York: Vintage Books

Kovach, Bill, and Tom Rosenstiel. 2007. *The Elements of Journalism: What Newspeople Should Know and the Public Should Expect.* New York: Three Rivers Press (1st publ. 2001)

Lashmar, Paul. 2011. *The Future of Investigative Journalism: Reasons to Be Cheerful.* OpenDemocracy UK, 13 June. https://www.opendemocracy.net/ourkingdom/paul-lashmar/future-of-investigative-journalism-reasons-to-be-cheerful (Accessed July 2017).

Lashmar, Paul. 2014. 'From the Insight Team to Wikileaks: The Continuing Power of Investigative Journalism as a Benchmark of Quality News Journalism', in Peter J. Anderson, Michael Williams, and George Ogola (eds), *The Future of Quality News Journalism: A Cross-Continental Analysis*, 43–8. London: Routledge

Leigh, D. 2013. *Wikileaks: Inside Julian Assange's War on Secrecy.* London: Guardian Faber

Lewis, Charles. 2014. *935 Lies: The Future of Truth and the Decline of America's Moral Integrity.* New York: Public Affairs Books

Lewis, Charles, and the Center for Public Integrity. 1996. *The Buying of the President.* New York: HarperCollins/Avon

Lewis, Charles, Bill Allison, and the Center for Public Integrity. 2001. *The Cheating of America: How Tax Avoidance and Evasion by the Super Rich are Costing the Country Billions – and What You Can Do about it.* New York: HarperCollins.

Lih, Andrew. 2009. *The Wikipedia Revolution: How a Bunch of Nobodies*

Created the World's Greatest Encyclopedia. Foreword by Jimmy Wales. New York: Hyperion

Mair, J. and R. Keeble, eds. 2011. *Investigative Journalism: Dead or Alive?* London: Abramis

Meyer, Gitte, and Anker Brink Lund. 2008. 'International Language Monism and Homogenisation of Journalism', *Javnost – The Public*, 15/4: 73–86

Meyer, Philip. 2002. *Precision Journalism: A Reporter's Introduction to Social Science Methods.* Lanham, MD: Rowman & Littlefield Publishers (4th edn)

Millar, Gavin, and Andrew Scott. 2016. *Newsgathering.* Oxford: Oxford University Press

Morris, Jim. 2012. 'Asbestos deaths bring 16-year sentence', ICIJ. 13 Feb. https://www.icij.org/project/dangers-dust/asbestos-deaths-bring-16-year-sentence

Mungiu-Pippidi, A. 2015. *The Quest for Good Governance.* Cambridge: Cambridge University Press.

Newsroom Panama. 2015. 'From Modest Rented Home to Multi-Million Dollar Mansion', 15 Apr., http://www.newsroompanama.com/news/panama/from-modest-rented-home-to-multi-million-dollar-mansion

Nieman Foundation. 2009–10. 'NGOs and the News', NiemanLab. http://www.niemanlab.org/ngo/

Nhan, Johnny, Laura Huey, and Ryan Broll, 'Digilantism: An Analysis of Crowdsourcing and the Boston Marathon Bombings', *British Journal of Criminology* (Centre for Crime and Justice Studies, Dec. 2015): 341–61

Obermaier, F., and B. Obermayer. 2017. *The Panama Papers: Breaking the Story of How the Rich and Powerful Hide their Money.* London: Oneworld

OCCRP. 2017. 'Son of President of Equatorial Guinea on Trial in Paris for Embezzlement', 20 June, https://www.occrp.org/en/daily/6610-son-of-president-of-equatorial-guinea-on-trial-in-paris-for-embezzling

Onuoha, Mimi, Jeanne Pinder, and Jan Schaffer. 2015. *Guide to Crowdsourcing*, Nov. https://www.cjr.org/tow_center_reports/guide_to_crowdsourcing.php

OSF. 2017. *Legal Remedies for Grand Corruption – France's Biens Mal Acquis Affair: Lessons from a Decade of Legal Struggle.* Open Society Justice Initiative and Oxford University's Institute for Ethics, Law and Armed Conflict. https://www.opensocietyfoundations.org/sites/default/files/legal-remedies-11-perdriel-20170612.pdf

Powers, Matthew. 2015. 'Contemporary NGO–Journalist Relations:

Reviewing and Evaluating an Emergent Area of Research', *Sociology Compass* 9/6: 427–37

Poynter. 2016. 'ASNE Stops Trying to Count Total Job Losses in American Newsrooms', 9 Sept., https://www.poynter.org/2016/asne-stops-trying-to-count-total-job-losses-in-american-newsrooms/429515

Prensa, la. 2017. 'Judicial Case Against Ricardo Martinelli: From Boss to Grandpa Chased and Sick', 20 June. http://impresa.prensa.com/panorama/mandamas-abuelito-perseguido-enfermo_0_4783771694.html

Prisma. 2015. 'The Scandalous Corruption in Panama under Martinelli (II)', 25 Jan., http://theprisma.co.uk/2015/01/25/the-scandalous-corruption-in-panama-under-ricardo-martinelli-ii

Quartz. 2016. 'Dutch authorities have seized a $120 million luxury yacht from this African president's son'. https://qz.com/860194/equatorial-guineas-teodorin-obiang-has-had-his-luxury-yacht-seized-in-the-netherlands

Reese, Stephen D. 2007. 'Journalism Research and the Hierarchy of Influence Model: A Global Perspective', *Brazilian Journalism Research*, 3/2/2

Renzulli, Diane, and the Center for Public Integrity. 2002. *Capitol Offenders: How Private Interests Govern our States*. Washington, DC: Public Integrity Books

Reporters Without Borders. 2017. *Freedom of the Press Index*. https://rsf.org/en/2017-press-freedom-index-ever-darker-world-map

Rosen, Jay. 2010. 'The View from Nowhere', Pressthink.org, 10 Nov. http://pressthink.org/2010/11/the-view-from-nowhere-questions-and-answers

Rosen, Jay. 2016. 'Prospects for the American Press Under Trump, Part Two'. http://pressthink.org/2016/12/prospects-american-press-trump-part-two

Rusbridger, Alan. 2009. 'I've Seen the Future and it's Mutual', *British Journalism Review* 20/3 (Sept.): 19–26

Sambrook, Richard. 2012. *Delivering Trust: Impartiality and Objectivity in the Digital Age*. Oxford: Reuters Institute for the Study of Journalism. https://ora.ox.ac.uk/objects/uuid:65d540e2-22e7-4a9c-a766-62c4db2fa4c3/datastreams/ATTACHMENT01

Schwarzlose, Richard Allen. 1989. *The Nation's Newsbrokers: The Formative Years, from Pretelegraph to 1865*. Evanston, IL: Northwestern University Press

Stapenhurst, Rick. 2000. *The Media's Role in Curbing Corruption*. WBI working papers. Washington, DC: World Bank. http://documents.worldbank.org/curated/en/893191468766225068/The-medias-role-in-curbing-corruption

Starkman, D. 2014. *The Watchdog that Didn't Bark*. New York: Columbia University Press

Steele, Bob. 2010. 'The Dangers of Activist-Driven Journalism', CNN, 30 Sept. http://edition.cnn.com/2010/OPINION/09/30/steele.objective.journalism/index.html

Sullivan, Andrew. 2017. 'Interview: Disrupting the Kleptocrat's Playbook, One Investigative Report at a Time', PRI.org. https://www.pri.org/stories/2017-04-21/disrupting-kleptocrats-playbook-one-investigative-report-time

Surowiecki, James. 2004. *The Wisdom of Crowds: Why the Many are Smarter than the Few and How Collective Wisdom Shapes Business, Economies, Societies and Nations*. New York: Doubleday/Anchor

Transparency International. 2008. *Legal Complaint Against African Heads of State for Misappropriation of Public Assets: How Can NGOs Play a Role in Recovering Stolen Assets?* Paris: Transparency International

Transparency International. 2011. *How Can Civil Society Act to Obtain the Recovery of Misappropriated Assets?* Paris: Transparency International

Transparency International. 2012. Survey Series: 'Putting Corruption Out of Business'. https://www.transparency.org/news/feature/putting_corruption_out_of_business

Uslaner, Eric. 2008. *Corruption Inequality and the Rule of Law*. Cambridge: Cambridge University Press

Waisbord, Silvio. 2011. 'Can NGOs Change the News?', *International Journal of Communication* 5: 142–65. http://ijoc.org/index.php/ijoc/article/viewFile/787/515

Weinberg, Arthur, and Lila Shaffer-Weinberg, eds. 2001. *The Muckrakers*. Champaign, IL: University of Illinois Press

Weinberger, David. 2009. 'Transparency: The New Objectivity'. 28 Aug. KMWorld. http://www.kmworld.com/Articles/Column/David-Weinberger/Transparency-the-new-objectivity-55785.aspx

WHO. 2014. *Chrystotile Asbestos*. Geneva: WHO Press. http://www.who.int/ipcs/assessment/public_health/chrysotile_asbestos_summary.pdf

RISJ PUBLICATIONS